YORK NOTE

General Editors: Professor Æ
of Stirling) & Professor Suhᵢ
University of Beirut)

CW00349716

Henry Fielding

TOM JONES

Notes by Lance St John Butler

MA (CAMBRIDGE) PH D (STIRLING)
Lecturer in English Studies,
University of Stirling

LONGMAN
YORK PRESS

YORK PRESS
Immeuble Esseily, Place Riad Solh, Beirut.

LONGMAN GROUP LIMITED
Burnt Mill,
Harlow, Essex

© Librairie du Liban 1981

First published 1981
ISBN 0 582 78205 8
Printed in Hong Kong by
Sing Cheong Printing Co Ltd

Contents

Part 1

Introduction

The life of Henry Fielding

Henry Fielding was born in 1707 and died in 1754. Although he was by birth a gentleman (his grandfather was a judge, his father became a general in the army and he was educated at Eton), he had to earn his living throughout his adulthood. Between 1729, when he returned to London after a period at the University of Leyden in Holland, and 1737 he worked as a playwright and theatre manager. He specialised in farces and satires on contemporary politicians and it was because of these last that his career as a dramatist came to an end when, in 1737, Walpole, the Prime Minister and a main target of Fielding's satire, put a Theatre Licensing Act through parliament.

Immediately Fielding turned to the law as a profession. He had married his beloved Charlotte (the model for Sophia Western in *Tom Jones*) in 1734 and with some money inherited from her mother he studied for, and passed, his law examinations. The remainder of his life was divided between the law and non-dramatic literature.

As far as the legal side of his career is concerned there is as much success to relate as there is on the literary side. Although he did not do very well as a barrister he became a famous magistrate in Westminster and, with his half-brother John, was responsible for the organisation of a minimal police-force in London. He put his principles of honesty and mercy into effect as a Justice at a time when this was not always done.

In literature an event took place in 1740 which opened the door to a new career for Fielding not long after the theatre doors had been shut on him. This was the publication of Samuel Richardson's novel *Pamela*. Fielding worked throughout the second half of his adult life as a journalist and essayist but *Pamela* prompted him to become a novelist as well. Richardson's novel is about a servant-girl who ultimately forces her master into marrying her by refusing all his other advances. In fact Pamela is a good and kind girl, and her master comes to love her in the end (and, it has to be said, Fielding himself, after Charlotte's death in 1744, married one of her maids). However, there are elements of puritanism, of middle-class scheming and smugness in Richardson's handling of the matter and, certainly, it all takes far too long; this provoked Fielding into the issuing of a brief, anonymous tale entitled

Shamela (1741), in which the young woman's 'true' thoughts are revealed, and she is shown up as a cunning and amorous creature.

Fielding was obviously much taken with this theme, and in 1742 he published *Joseph Andrews*, a novel about Pamela's supposed brother in which the latter manages to preserve his chastity in spite of assaults on it by Lady Booby and others, much as Pamela preserves hers in Richardson's novel. Joseph Andrews is in some ways a prototype of Tom Jones and the novel to which he gives his name goes over much of the same moral ground as the later novel: Joseph is honest, courageous and generous; his companion, Parson Adams, is a picture of Christian simplicity.

In 1749 Fielding published his great work, *Tom Jones*. His publisher paid him a total of seven hundred pounds for the novel, an indication of its success and popularity.

In 1751 *Amelia* appeared, his last novel and one which, although unjustly neglected, shows less brilliance than its predecessors.

In 1754, after a journey to Lisbon, recorded in his *Journal of a Voyage to Lisbon*, Fielding died of gout and other diseases.

Literary background to *Tom Jones*

Fielding's life falls entirely within what is known as the 'Augustan' period of English literature and taste. Neo-classicism was at its height in the first half of the eighteenth century, and along with the elegance and refinement of this went a taste for vicious satire, wit and bawdiness.

The tone had been set in the last forty years of the seventeenth century (since the Restoration of Charles II in 1660 and the temporary defeat of puritanism). The theatres, which had been closed under Cromwell, came back to a very vigorous life, with women playing female roles for the first time. The satirical brilliance of Restoration comedy, often based on explicitly sexual themes, was balanced by some attempts at writing classical tragedy and by a 'classicisation' of earlier plays and plots.

Vanbrugh, Etherege, Wycherley, the Duke of Buckingham and others are among comic dramatists of this period mentioned by Fielding in *Tom Jones* (and imitated by him in his career as a playwright, 1729–37). In this context the master comedian Molière must be mentioned; his great plays all belong to the 1660s and he was something of a model for later writers.

On the tragic side, readers of *Tom Jones* will be aware of the names of Addison (1672–1719), whose neo-classical drama *Cato* (1713) is referred to Otway (1652–85), author of *The Orphan* (1680), Dryden (1631–1700) and Congreve (1670–1729).

Mention of Dryden brings us to satire and classicism outside the theatre. With his contemporaries Samuel Butler (1612–80) and the

Earl of Rochester (1648–80), both mentioned by Fielding, the former frequently, and his successors Pope and Swift, Dryden forms part of the school of Augustan satirists whose handling of barbed verse has not been equalled. These poets, in polished and civilised couplets, satirised with great effect the sometimes uncivilised behaviour of their contemporaries. When we consider Pope's dates (1688–1744) and Swift's (1667–1745) we can see that Fielding stands at the end of a long tradition and that he had many excellent models to draw on in the theatre and in poetry. We have already seen that he had *Pamela* to react against in the matter of prose fiction.

Pamela, however, was not the only novel to influence him. Fielding stood in the main stream of an early style of fiction partly summed up by the term 'picaresque'. This fiction has some origins in Greek and Latin literature (one can think of Odysseus, the hero of Homer's *Odyssey*, being driven around the known world by the wrath of the god Poseidon rather as Tom is driven about England by his fates) but for Fielding its great master was the Spanish writer Miguel de Cervantes, whose *Don Quixote* had appeared between 1605 and 1615. Other sources may be traced in this area, such as the French novels of Paul Scarron and Alain Le Sage (whose *Gil Blas* of 1715–35 was published in an English translation in 1749, the year of *Tom Jones*) but Cervantes stands out as Fielding's model. Tom is not like Don Quixote, of course, but the authorial method of inserting commentary into the action and the broadly satirical approach taken to each character as he or she is introduced show the debt clearly enough.

For more on the literary background to *Tom Jones*, see the Commentary in Part 3 of these Notes, especially the sections on Fielding and the theatre and Fielding and the classics.

A note on the text

Four editions of *Tom Jones* were published in 1749, although the last of them is dated 1750. They vary in a large number of details and good modern editions try to strike a balance between these variations, but there are no really substantial differences to be considered.

Between 1882 and 1926 five editions of Fielding appeared, all including *Tom Jones*, offering either the 'works' (for instance, Sir Leslie Stephen's edition of 1882) or the 'novels' (the Oxford edition of 1926).

More recent and more popular editions include the Everyman's Library edition of 1909 (frequently reprinted; now in soft covers with an introduction by A. R. Humphreys; 2 volumes) and the excellent Penguin edition of R. P. C. Mutter, complete with introduction, notes and glossary, of 1966 (frequently reprinted). These Notes follow Mutter's text, including his retention of Fielding's spelling.

Part 2

Summaries
of TOM JONES

A general summary

The eighteen books of *Tom Jones* are divided into three sections of six
books each. In the first section (Books 1–6) Tom is born (or found) and
brought up to manhood at Mr Allworthy's. We learn of the past histories and present dispositions of Allworthy, Blifil and the others at
Paradise Hall, also of Squire Western and Sophia. At the end of this
section Tom is in love with Sophia (and she with him) but is expelled
from home for supposed bad behaviour. Blifil has poisoned Allworthy's
mind against Tom and Tom has been caught out in an affair with Molly
Seagrim. He feels he could not, in any case, court Sophia as he is poor
and her father wants her to marry Blifil.

In the second section (Books 7–12) everybody goes on their travels.
Tom, with Partridge, decides first to go to sea and, later, to join the
army. Sophia and Honour leave home as running away to London
seems to be the only way of avoiding Sophia's marriage to Blifil. Tom
and Sophia nearly coincide several times and when, in the end, Sophia,
in the company of Mrs Fitzpatrick, travels directly to London in the
Irish peer's coach, Tom and Partridge follow, encountering adventures
(such as brawls) and people (such as the Man of the Hill) on the way.
Squire Western has set out in pursuit of his daughter and nearly catches
her. Meanwhile all England is in an uproar about the 1745 Jacobite
rebellion.

In the third section (Books 13–18) everybody gathers in London.
Tom takes lodgings, where he meets and helps one Nightingale, and
lives guiltily off his affair with Lady Bellaston while searching for
Sophia. Sophia stays with various people until she is caught by her
father who, together with her aunt, tries to force her to accept Blifil
while Lady Bellaston tries to force her to accept Lord Fellamar. Mr
Allworthy and Blifil come to town and the scene is set for an ending.
Gradually the treachery of Blifil becomes known, Allworthy takes Tom
back into his favour, Western is pleased to marry his daughter to
whomever will inherit from Allworthy, Tom is forgiven his infidelities
and he and Sophia are married.

Detailed summaries

Epigraph

'He saw the manners of many men': a quotation from the Latin poet Horace (65-8BC). He is writing about Odysseus, also called Ulysses, the first tourist, hero of Homer's epic poem, the *Odyssey*

Dedication

Fielding explains his four main aims in writing this novel:
(1) To make men admire the beauty of virtue.
(2) To show that happiness ('comfort of mind') gained through virtue cannot be compensated for by anything gained immorally (that is, the virtuous are happier than the vicious).
(3) To show that acquiring things immorally is dangerous and often unsuccessful.
(4) To show that virtuous people, if they keep their wits about them, will almost never suffer injury (that is, virtue is a shield).

NOTES AND GLOSSARY:

George Lyttleton: (1709–73), a friend and patron of Fielding's. Later Chancellor of the Exchequer

A particular acquaintance: Ralph Allen (1694–1764), a rich friend and patron of Fielding's. The model for Mr Allworthy

The Duke of Bedford: John Russell, fourth duke (1710–71), a patron of Fielding's

A great poet: Alexander Pope (1688–1744), the great satiric poet

Plato: (427–348BC), Greek philosopher

Book 1 Chapter 1

(Notice that each book opens with a chapter of prologue in which Fielding discusses things literary with the reader.)

This novel is a feast at which the food is 'Human Nature'. Fielding will 'dress up' the plain facts about human nature with various kinds of sauces.

NOTES AND GLOSSARY:

foundling: orphan child abandoned by its parents and found by someone else

bill of fare: menu

eleemosynary:	charitable, given free of charge
ordinary:	public eating-house
d–n:	throughout *Tom Jones* Fielding employs the old-fashioned device of omitting the central letters from obscene or profane words. Here the word partly concealed is 'damn'
regale:	feast
victuallers:	sellers of food
calibash and calipee:	delicacies; parts of the turtle
viands:	food
Bayonne ham or Bologna sausage:	ham and sausage, from these towns in France and Italy respectively, of the highest quality
Mr Pope:	See General glossary
Heliogabalus:	a Roman emperor (ruled AD218–22) noted for his gluttony and libertinism
Hash and ragoo:	to hash is to crush or mash up food. To 'ragoo' (nowadays 'ragout') is to serve food as a spicy stew

Book 1 Chapter 2

This chapter gives a brief description of Mr Allworthy and his sister Bridget.

NOTES AND GLOSSARY:

Somersetshire:	a county in the south-west of England
Allworthy:	notice the meaning implied by this name. *Is* he 'all-worthy'? Is he like God, as that would suggest? He does, after all, live at 'Paradise Hall'. Notice other significant names such as those of Thwackum (roughly, 'beat-them') and Square (refers to the 'rule of right' by which this philosopher lives and by which he tries to 'square' human behaviour)
person:	body and face (not personality)
aera:	era; period
trained bands:	militia; citizens' army
I intend to digress:	notice Fielding's freedom to digress, to talk directly to the reader, to comment on the action. He defends himself in this bold statement against the classically minded critic who might try to insist on the Aristotelian 'unity of action' which would prevent digression
judges . . . jurisdiction:	Fielding was a magistrate and he often uses legal terminology, as here

Book 1 Chapter 3

Tom is found, a baby, in Mr Allworthy's bed.

NOTES AND GLOSSARY:

'The History of England': various publications with this sort of title may be the target of Fielding's satire here, for instance, John Lockman's *History of England* (1735) or Thomas Carte's *General History* (1747)

matron: older woman

Mrs Deborah Wilkins: 'Mrs' was a courtesy title for older women and did not necessarily imply that they were married. 'Mrs Deborah' is single

sluts . . . strumpets: terms of insult implying sexual immorality on the part of the women against whom they are directed

misbegotten: either 'born mistakenly' or 'born out of wedlock' (a bastard)

pap: food for babies; milk and water with bread

place: position as a servant, employment

Book 1 Chapter 4

Allworthy's house is described. He tells Bridget of Tom. She reacts.

NOTES AND GLOSSARY:

Gothick . . . Grecian: Romantic art and architecture began to rival classical styles only in the middle of the eighteenth century, so Fielding, writing in the 1740s, may seem to be before his time in giving Mr Allworthy a 'Gothick' (Romantic) house. However, in the usage of Fielding's England, 'Gothic' (or 'Gothick') can be taken simply to mean 'medieval', 'pre-renaissance' or 'pre-neoclassical'. 'Grecian' simply implies 'classical'. The taste for the wild, the romantic and the Gothic was closely associated with a preference for uncultivated nature and irregular scenery. This is associated, for instance, with the poetry of Wordsworth (1770–1850), Scott (1771–1832) and their contemporaries (Wordsworth and Coleridge's *Lyrical Ballads* which set some of the tone of this 'Romantic' period were published in 1798) but the earlier eighteenth century had its 'Gothic' side and a romantic interest in nature as is exemplified in the poetry of Fielding's close contemporary, James Thomson. The third paragraph of this chapter is another example of this early Romanticism. Notice the cascade, described as 'not carried down a *regular* flight of steps, but tumbling in a *natural* fall over the *broken* and mossy stones' (present author's italics)

prospect: view

owing less to art than to nature: this is a constant theme in the eighteenth century, as it is in classical and renaissance literature. Notice the contrast in *Tom Jones* between the country (nature) and the town (art). The system of values in the novel is in part an exploration of this division

Reader, take care . . .: Fielding creates an ironic detachment from his story by bringing the artificial nature of fiction-writing to our attention

Complacence: the desire to please (not pejorative)

Condescension: kindness to an inferior (not pejorative)

Slut . . . hussy . . . harlot . . . jade . . . strumpet: terms of insult implying sexual immorality on the part of the women against whom they are directed

---

Book 1 Chapter 5

Miss Bridget Allworthy takes charge of Tom.

NOTES AND GLOSSARY:
Notice how Fielding hints at Tom's parentage in his description of Miss Allworthy's treatment of him. 'Her orders were indeed so liberal, that, *had it been a child of her own*, she could not have exceeded them.' (Present author's italics.)

Book 1 Chapter 6

Mrs Deborah accuses Jenny Jones of being Tom's mother. Jenny confesses. She is described.

NOTES AND GLOSSARY:
not otherwise than when a kite . . .: see note on epic similes in Part 3, Commentary, pp.101-2

she obtained a very competent skill in the Latin language . . .: see section on classical learning in Part 3, Commentary

relish: here, taste

In embrio: in embryo, in a preparatory and immature condition

felicitated: congratulated
trollops: girls of easy virtue
House of Correction: prison-like institution for the reformation of criminals, especially prostitutes and the like

Book 1 Chapter 7

Mr Allworthy gives a sermon to Jenny on chastity. Note that Allworthy is not so all-knowing that he can see through Jenny's story, which turns out to be false.

NOTES AND GLOSSARY:
sophistry: clever but spurious arguments
bubble: someone who is the victim of cheating
decent: modest
stagger: to trip up
ingenuity: here, ingenuousness

Book 1 Chapter 8

Mrs Deborah and Miss Bridget discuss this sermon and the matter of Jenny Jones.

NOTES AND GLOSSARY:
'de non apparentibus . . .': (*Latin*) what does not appear does not exist
Homer: Greek epic poet; see General glossary and the note on classical learning in Part 3, Commentary
Venus: the Roman goddess of love
Lady Seraphina: Fielding is not necessarily thinking of any lady in particular here; he refers to any lady of fashion
Tysiphone: one of the three Furies in Greek Myth, forces of vengeance and cruelty
Boreas: the north wind in classical legend
seamed with the smallpox: smallpox was once a widespread disease; it could leave the face scarred permanently

Book 1 Chapter 9

How the village reacts when it hears that Jenny is not to go to the House of Correction. A discussion of the good sense of not punishing her.

NOTES AND GLOSSARY:
beating hemp: working in a prison
Bridewell: a London prison of the period

Book 1 Chapter 10

Dr Blifil and his brother are received by Mr Allworthy.

NOTES AND GLOSSARY:

you was sure to gain a dinner: notice the freedom Fielding has to use 'you was' or 'you were'. Both were correct

Touchstone: a stone used to reveal whether a metal is gold or not, that is, a test

the Roman kalendar: the Catholic list of saints and their feast-days

criminal correspondence: here, illicit sexual relations

deposit: here, put aside

He had purchased the post of lieutenant of dragoons: from the seventeenth century to the middle of the nineteenth century the normal way of obtaining a commission in the army was to buy it. Merit only rarely took precedence over money

rusticated: gone to live in the country

Methodism: the Methodists were a religious group originally within the Church of England founded by the brothers John Wesley (1703-91) and Charles Wesley (1707-80) together with Charles Whitefield (1714-70) in 1729. They tended towards a Bible-based Christianity, Puritanism and Calvinism. In 1795 they split off from the Church of England. To such as Fielding they were poor creatures, narrow-minded and self-righteous, lacking in generosity of spirit. Note the fate of Blifil junior in the last chapter of the novel—he becomes a Methodist 'in hopes of marrying a very rich widow of that sect'

Ovid: Publius Ovidius Naso (43BC-AD18), Roman poet

Book 1 Chapter 11

There is a discussion of love. Captain Blifil is seen to have designs on Miss Bridget and her fortune. Notice how at the end of this chapter Mr Allworthy is again deceived; but then he does not have 'the insight of the devil'.

NOTES AND GLOSSARY:

distemper: here, disease; her 'temper' has not been *dis*-turbed

chairman: several times in this novel people travel by 'chair'. A 'chair' or 'sedan-chair' was a carriage with a single seat and no wheels, in which the passenger sat and which was then carried by two men. These men ('chairmen') had to be strong and the reference to their legs here is to establish the size and strength of Captain Blifil

a much prettier fellow: notice that 'pretty' can be applied to men in eighteenth-century English

Mr Hogarth ... A Winter's Morning: William Hogarth (1697–1764) was a major artist of the period, specialising in satirical prints, and a friend of Fielding's. His print of 'Morning' of 1736 from a series called *Four Times of the Day* shows a tall, thin, plain woman on her way to Covent Garden Church, in London, looking disapprovingly at some young lovers

nicety: fastidiousness; care

tenements and hereditaments: those things which a man holds, and which he has inherited and can bequeath

the Witch of Endor: a hideous old woman (see the Bible, I Samuel 28:7)

'nolo episcopari': (*Latin*) 'I do not wish to be a bishop'. The traditional reply first given to the royal offer of a bishopric which is then accepted. The phrase implies a pretended unwillingness

Book 1 Chapter 12

With his brother's help, Captain Blifil manages to ensnare Miss Bridget.

NOTES AND GLOSSARY:
'sui juris': (*Latin*) in charge of her own affairs
lenity: leniency
panegyric ... encomiums: praise
Scripture: the Bible, Old and New Testaments
equipage: equipment but, particularly, horses and carriages

Book 1 Chapter 13

Captain Blifil drives his brother away from Mr Allworthy's.

NOTES AND GLOSSARY:
bill of mortality: list of those who have died

Book 2 Chapter 1

Fielding explains the sort of 'history' he is writing, saying he wants to highlight significant episodes and pass quickly over less important ones.

NOTES AND GLOSSARY:

properly: appropriately

apology: here, explanation; vindication. Fielding is probably satirising Colley Cibber (1671–1757), the actor and playwright, whose *Apology* appeared in 1740

aeras: (*Latin*) eras

amanuensis: scholarly assistant

the excellent Latin poet: Lucretius (*c*.99–55BC). The lines come from his most famous work *On the Nature of Things (De Rerum Natura)*, translated by Thomas Creech (1659–1700)

lottery: in the state lotteries held throughout the eighteenth century the tickets which won nothing were blanks

Guild-hall: the Guildhall is the traditional administrative centre of the City of London

'jure divino': (*Latin*) divine law; here, divine right

commodity: in eighteenth-century English, a quantity or parcel of something

---

Book 2 Chapter 2

Captain Blifil wants Tom sent away, but Mr Allworthy insists on charity. Notice the total lack of charity in Captain Blifil's quoting of Scripture.

NOTES AND GLOSSARY:

bred up together: in Fielding's day (and later) 'breeding', especially when used of human beings, referred to education rather than to the genetic results of mating

the lowest and vilest offices of the commonwealth: the worst jobs in society

parabolically: as a parable

oeconomy: economy, the organisation or infrastructure of something; not necessarily to do with its financial aspect

---

Book 2 Chapter 3

Mr and Mrs Partridge are described, and the story is told of the dismissal of Jenny Jones.

NOTES AND GLOSSARY:

Aristotle: (384–322BC) Greek philosopher. In the title to this chapter it is the 'description' (rather than the

'domestic Government') which is contrary to the
'Rules' of Aristotle as laid down in his *Poetics*

emolument: financial reward

Eton or Westminster: two of the oldest and most famous British public
(private) schools

syntaxis: a Latin grammar-book which should have been
studied long before the pupil was seventeen years
old

parish-boys: poor boys being supported by local charity

Hogarth: see note to Book 1 Chapter 11, above

the Harlot's Progress: a series of satirical prints by Hogarth, completed
in 1732, showing stages in the life of a prostitute

Xantippe: wife of the Athenian philosopher Socrates, famous
for her bad temper and nagging

'Da mihi aliquid potum': (*Latin*) give me something to drink

trencher: wooden plate

Othello: Othello (in Shakespeare's play) is the great example
of jealousy

Book 2 Chapter 4

Mrs Partridge learns that Jenny has had two bastard children. She
attacks her husband.

NOTES AND GLOSSARY:

Free Masonry: the Freemasons are a partly secret society of
Protestants whose aim is to assist one another in
political and commercial ways

Nemesis: the classical goddess of retribution

invidious: full of envy

Mr John Fr—: John Freke (1688–1756), an early experimenter
with electricity. The word 'philosopher' was used
in the eighteenth century to mean 'scientist' as well
as 'abstract thinker'

descanting: talking a great deal

Horace: Quintus Horatius Flaccus (65–8BC), Roman poet

coffee-houses: drinking establishments. These were the places of
resort of writers, talkers, businessmen, during the
seventeenth and eighteenth centuries. They were
centres of gossip, discussion and trade

chandler's shop: approximately, 'the grocer's'; chandlers sold pro-
visions of all sorts

overseer: here, parish officer in charge of charity, for instance
the care of abandoned bastards

journeymen:	workers paid by the day; the stage after apprentice-ship
Grimalkin:	a traditional name for a cat
redundant:	here, excessive in size
Amazonian:	the Amazons were a tribe of female warriors supposedly overcome by Theseus in the Greek myths
'una voce':	(*Latin*) with one voice

Book 2 Chapter 5

Captain Blifil, on learning that Partridge is accused of being Tom's father, 'generously' acquaints Mr Allworthy with this.

NOTES AND GLOSSARY:

transpire:	here, be talked about further abroad
charity:	notice Captain Blifil's horrible version of this virtue. See the section on 'good nature' in Part 3, Commentary
epicures:	those who delight in pleasure, especially in the pleasure of eating (see note to Book 15 Chapter 1 on p.79)
largesses:	charitable donations
enthusiasm:	in the eighteenth century this word was pejorative, especially in connection with religion where it was used to describe a kind of low-church fanaticism that was considered vulgar and dangerous. Thus, at the end of Allworthy's speech in this chapter 'atheism, or enthusiasm' are presented as equal evils

---

Book 2 Chapter 6

Partridge is tried and convicted of Tom's paternity by Allworthy. He loses his annuity.

NOTES AND GLOSSARY:

'viva voce':	(*Latin*) orally
Paradise Hall:	notice the implications of the name of Mr Allworthy's residence
Mrs Partridge:	she speaks incorrectly, employing malapropisms such as 'commandiments' (for 'commandments') and 'bullocking' (for 'bullying'). Fielding is a master of the art of revealing character through speech. See the note on this in Part 3, Commentary

taxed: here, accused

a certain learned author: Sir Edward Coke (1552–1634), the great Elizabethan lawyer

tho' I called him, poor Partridge: in this typically Fieldingesque aside to the reader, the author points out that he has cleverly not revealed to us whether Partridge is guilty or not

would have taken the sacrament upon the matter: would have sworn upon the Holy Eucharist, the bread of the communion service

exquisite: extreme, exact, refined

Book 2 Chapter 7

The hatred of Captain and Mrs Blifil for one another is described.

NOTES AND GLOSSARY:

complaisance: friendliness

Hoadly: Bishop Benjamin Hoadly (1676–1761) was involved in controversy about the divine authority of kings, which is another aspect of the problem of authority under discussion here

condescension: see General glossary

Aristotle: this philosopher held woman to be naturally inferior to man. See General glossary

toying: kissing and cuddling

with a degree of folly which we can deceive: with people sufficiently foolish that we can deceive them (into believing that we are without faults)

Book 2 Chapter 8

Captain Blifil dies.

NOTES AND GLOSSARY:

reversions: property known to be bequeathed to someone and therefore having a cash value to that person even while the testator is still living

'mal-a-propos':   (*French*) irrelevant; untimely

Fielding refers to 'Fortune', with a capital letter, thus following the classical custom of personifying and even deifying abstract entities. (Compare this with 'Death', in the next chapter, who is an 'inexorable judge'.)

Book 2 Chapter 9

Mrs Blifil is in hysterics and the doctors dispute uselessly. Notice
Fielding's use of single words to act as ironic pins pricking the balloons
 of pretence and pretension, for instance, 'after the fit had continued a
decent time' and 'all the *decorations* of sickness'. Notice the irony of
Captain Blifil's epitaph. The qualities here mentioned are a partial
summary of Fielding's values.

NOTES AND GLOSSARY:
dropping: applying drops of medicine
the stone, the gravel: disorders of the kidneys and bladder
scarified: treated with a series of cuts

Book 3 Chapter 1

Time has gone by. Tom is now fourteen years old.

NOTES AND GLOSSARY:
weeds: clothes worn by recent widows

Book 3 Chapter 2

Tom poaches with the gamekeeper. He is courageous in not revealing
the gamekeeper's identity, even though he is beaten by Thwackum.
Notice the careful presentation, in the early paragraphs of this chapter,
of Tom and Blifil, side by side. The moral issues are made very clear.

NOTES AND GLOSSARY:
'meum' and 'tuum': (*Latin*) mine and thine
that atrocious wickedness in Jones: we know that we are not meant to
                think of Tom as really wicked because of the
                exaggeration of the adjective
an accessory after the fact: one who assists in a crime after it has hap-
                pened (for example, a receiver of stolen goods)
bannians: a strictly vegetarian caste of Hindus

Book 3 Chapter 3

Thwackum and Square dispute over a trivial point. Square regards 'all
virtue as matter of theory only'. This was one of Fielding's particular
hatreds; see the section on 'good nature' in Part 3, Commentary.
Notice the pedantry, pettiness, selfishness and arrogance of these two
learned gentlemen.

NOTES AND GLOSSARY:

Thwackum and Square: see the note on 'Allworthy' in the notes to Book 1 Chapter 2, above. These two stereotypes are said to be modelled on two of Fielding's contemporaries

his natural parts: 'parts' were a man's abilities, chiefly intellectual

Plato and Aristotle: see General glossary

Coke upon Lyttleton: a legal text-book, published in 1628

Book 3 Chapter 4

This chapter reveals much of Tom's character through his relationship with Blifil, and the contrast between them. Tom is 'inoffensive' *and* 'passionate' (not given to hurting people *and* likely to fly into a temper).

NOTES AND GLOSSARY:

Notice Fielding's occasional indulgence in less usual words, such as 'obviate' and 'profligate', usually of Latin origin.

the bands of civil society: the 'bonds'; what holds society together

natural goodness of heart: a very important theme in Fielding's work. See the section on 'good nature' in Part 3, Commentary

affirmance: affirmation

Book 3 Chapter 5

Thwackum and Square discuss Tom's behaviour. Black George is dismissed. Blifil is shown to be a hypocrite. Towards the end of this chapter Fielding specifically defends Mr Allworthy against the charge, which is often made, of his being blind to the real characters of those around him.

NOTES AND GLOSSARY:

lashing: beating

birch: rods for beating schoolboys were generally made of this wood

Solomon: King of Israel in the tenth century BC, famous for his wisdom

---

Book 3 Chapter 6

This chapter tells of the rivalry between Thwackum and Square for the affections of Mrs Blifil (Mr Allworthy's sister).

NOTES AND GLOSSARY:

'Expressum facit . . .': (*Latin*) what is expressed suppresses what is only silently understood

flea: an old spelling of 'flay'

Harlot's Progress: a famous series of prints; see General glossary, under Hogarth

Bridewel(l): see General glossary

Book 3 Chapter 7

A discourse on virtue, which should *appear* as well as *be*. Mr Allworthy starts to dislike Tom, in compensation for his sister's neglect of Blifil.

NOTES AND GLOSSARY:

glass: here, telescope

the rocks on which innocence and goodness often split: to split, here, means to be wrecked, as in a ship 'splitting'. The idea is that innocence and goodness are *both* wrecked; it does not mean that they are split off from one another

---

Book 3 Chapter 8

Tom sells his horse to support the gamekeeper, a demonstration of his good nature.

NOTES AND GLOSSARY:

smart-money: money which was paid to soldiers for the wounds they received

smarting: hurting

farthing: a coin, a quarter of an old penny

Book 3 Chapter 9

Tom sells a Bible and continues to help Black George. Notice Fielding's careful arrangement of the moral issues here. Tom sells a *Bible*, the very book which enjoins us to help the poor, to get money to help the poor. Blifil uses the same book to get Tom into trouble by reading it often and drawing it to everyone's attention. Thus one boy is truly Christian while appearing to contravene some of the more superficial Christian standards, while the other boy gains a reputation for Christian virtue (and a cheap Bible) by performing uncharitable and ungrateful actions. The reactions of Allworthy, Thwackum and Square round off this moral pantomime.

NOTES AND GLOSSARY:

Tillotson's sermons: John Tillotson (1630–94) was Archbishop of Canterbury; his *Sermons* were extremely popular and ran into many editions

Book 3 Chapter 10

Black George falls foul of the game laws again; Tom is popular with Squire Western.

NOTES AND GLOSSARY:

form: the 'bed' in which a hare lies in the grass

the laws of the land: this is in reference to the Game Laws (1671 and 1691) which excluded everyone except the rich from killing game, even on their own land. The laws were weighted heavily in favour of the squires (landowners), who upheld them fiercely

higler: pedlar, travelling dealer in various commodities, including game

wired: caught in wire traps

leaping over five-barred gates: Tom's abilities, here referred to, are equestrian; the leaping is that of a 'sportsman', a man on horseback

sport: note the change in meaning of this word. In the eighteenth century (and even in the nineteenth) its first meaning was connected with what we now call 'field-sports', hunting, shooting and fishing (not football or tennis). Fielding normally uses it in this way, especially when writing of Squire Western. Western is, in fact, a caricature of the 'sporting' squire

Book 4 Chapter 1

This chapter is about prefaces and the creation of suspense and prepares for the appearance of Sophia.

NOTES AND GLOSSARY:

the sole use of the pastry-cook: pastrycooks used the paper from unsold books as lining for their dishes

Butler: Samuel Butler (1612–80), one of Fielding's favourite authors, author of the satirical poem *Hudibras*, refers to writers being inspired by ale. (*Hudibras* Part 1, Canto 1, lines 645 ff.)

'Hurlothrumbo': an extravagant and wild play by Samuel Johnson of Cheshire (1691–1773)—not *the* great Dr Samuel Johnson (1709–84)

Homer: see General glossary

Jove: (Zeus in Greek; Jupiter or Jove in Latin) the father of the gods

this heroic, historical, prosaic poem: an echo of Fielding's famous definition of his earlier work, *Joseph Andrews*, which he describes as 'a comic epic poem in prose'. The point is that 'heroic', or epic, here means the opposite of 'historical', and 'prosaic' contradicts 'poem' just as 'comic' contradicts 'epic'. Fielding is playing with the notions of classical elevation and grandeur and claiming, half-seriously, that his modern prose comedy has some affinity with classical epic; which it has—see the section on Fielding's debt to the classics in Part 3, Commentary, pp.100–3, for a fuller discussion of these ideas

bombast and fustian: these metaphorical terms, taken from the world of clothing, were clichés in the eighteenth century denoting respectively a loud, ranting style (of acting) and a dull, homely style

Mr Lock's blind man: John Locke (1632–1704) proposes in his *Essay concerning Human Understanding* that we can learn about how we learn about things by considering how they would appear to those who do not have our knowledge of them

King Pyrrhus . . .: this story is told of a production of *Distrest Mother* by Ambrose Phipps (1675–1749) produced in 1712. Barton Booth (1681–1733) played Pyrrhus at Drury Lane, a theatre which he managed with Robert Wilks (1665–1732) and Colley Cibber 1671–1757)

the antients . . . Flora: 'the ancients' refers to the Greeks and Romans; Flora was the goddess of flowers

---

Book 4 Chapter 2

Sophia is described. Notice the elevated style of this description which imitates Homer and Virgil (70–19BC), author of the Latin epic, the *Aeneid*, and also some of the more exalted writers of the Renaissance. 'Sophia' is Greek for 'wisdom'.

Notice the relationship between nature and art discussed in the last paragraph of this chapter. See the notes to Book 1 Chapter 4, above.

NOTES AND GLOSSARY:
Boreas ... Eurus ... Zephyrus: respectively the north, east and west winds
Handel: the great composer (1685-1759) who settled permanently in England in 1712
Venus de Medicis: a statue of Venus, kept during Fielding's time in the Medici Palace in Rome
Hampton Court: built by Cardinal Wolsey and appropriated by Henry VIII in the 1530s; a royal residence throughout the eighteenth century. Twelve paintings of court beauties by Kneller were placed in the palace by Queen Mary
each bright Churchill: presumably the four beautiful daughters of John Churchill, Duke of Marlborough (1650-1722), painted by Sir Godfrey Kneller (1646-1723)
Kit-cat: a Whig club founded in 1700 (to be a 'toast' meant, of a woman, that the men drank to her beauty)
Lord Rochester: (1648-80) a Restoration poet, wit and libertine
Lady Ranelagh ... Duchess of Mazarine: beauties of the day
one whose image can never depart from my breast: Fielding seems to be referring to his wife, whom he loved passionately
Sir John Suckling: (1609-42), a Royalist poet and playwright
Dr Donne: John Donne (1571-1631), the great poet and preacher

Book 4 Chapter 3

Sophia's bird escapes, thanks to Blifil's malice; Tom tries to catch it. A contrast is drawn between the two boys. Notice that Sophia calls her bird 'Tommy'. This is an early sign of her love.

Book 4 Chapter 4

Thwackum, Square and Western give their opinions on the incident of the bird to Mr Allworthy. Their different positions are most revealing. Notice Square's catch-phrases, satirising the Deistical thinking of the day: 'the rule of right, and the eternal fitness of things'; also the almost incomprehensible jargon of the lawyer.

NOTES AND GLOSSARY:
meridian: noon; high point
the elder or the younger Brutus: Romans renowned for their honesty and strength of purpose. However, as the subsequent discussion of these two between Thwackum and

Square shows, their noble actions (one executed his own sons and the other murdered Julius Caesar) can be seen as unchristian and immoral

a deist or an atheist: deists held that God had revealed himself in the laws of nature and that Revelation (the Bible and the Church) was therefore redundant

pox of your laws of nature: here, as frequently later, Squire Western swears. 'Pox' (venereal disease) was an extremely common way of swearing in the eighteenth century. The full idea can thus be expressed as: 'May a nasty disease attack . . .'

tenets: ideas; things held as true; principles

philosophical cant: jargon; nonsense, usually hypocritical

mew: confined area for breeding birds

'ferae naturae': (*Latin*) of a wild nature; not tame

'nullius in bonis': (*Latin*) belonging to nobody

'nullus bonus': (*Latin*) no good to anyone

Book 4 Chapter 5

Tom and Sophia talk together. Tom asks her to intercede on behalf of Black George, which she does. Notice the effect of Tom's first kiss with Sophia. Fielding is fully aware of the physical effects.

NOTES AND GLOSSARY:

crying roast-meat: boasting prematurely of one's good fortune

gallantry: fornication (see the famous line by Lord Byron (1788-1824), the romantic poet, in his *Don Juan*: 'What men call gallantry and gods adultery')

Old Sir Simon . . .: these are all old English songs

sparks: 'spark' is still used in this familiar way to mean little more than 'chap' or 'fellow' but Fielding adds meaning to it by using the adjective 'ardent' later in the sentence

ardent: burning

Book 4 Chapter 6

Tom's relationship with Molly Seagrim is exposed and explained. In Fielding a good open character is often marked by a vigorous sexual appetite. Contrast Blifil's desire for Sophia with Tom's, for instance. See the section on 'good nature' in Part 3, Commentary.

Fielding involves his readers again in the opening of this chapter. Which side is the reader on?

NOTES AND GLOSSARY:

determination: here, decision

trunk-maker: a well-known character who attended plays in the earlier eighteenth century; he was known as a great applauder

explode: to boo; opposite of 'applaud'

the Lord High Chancellor: this comparison between the law within (conscience) and the law without (the Law) comes close to Fielding's ideal as a magistrate and moral man. Both laws exist to check the natural impulses of man. Thus Fielding says of Tom's love for Molly, 'this affection he had fixed on the girl long before he could bring himself to attempt the possession of her person: for tho' his *constitution* urged him greatly to this, his *principles* no less forcibly restrained him' (present author's italics)

Book 4 Chapter 7

The new dress Molly wears provokes envy and violence.

NOTES AND GLOSSARY:

vestry ... conclave: a contrast of small with large: even the smallest church has a vestry, where the priest puts on his robes, while a conclave is a gathering of all the senior bishops of a Church, notably a meeting of cardinals in Rome

Book 4 Chapter 8

A fight in the churchyard is provoked by Molly's dress. Notice the title of this chapter with its promise of classical imitation; 'taste' here means 'appreciate'. Notice the debt to Homer, Virgil, Milton and, perhaps, Cervantes in the mock-epic description of the battle. The trivial and unheroic nature of the encounter makes this style highly amusing from the Invocation ('Ye Muses then . . .') through the Epic Simile ('As a vast herd of cows . . .') to the list of fallen heroes ('Recount, O Muse . . .').

Molly Seagrim's pregnancy is made quite clear in this chapter ('her present unhappy condition').

Notice the Somersetshire accent of the countryman who answers Blifil. Generally speaking, if one pronounces this sort of dialect out loud in a stage west-country accent one can get the gist of what is being said easily enough.

NOTES AND GLOSSARY:

Homerican: the normal adjective used in reference to Homer is 'Homeric'

sack: here, dress

certain missile weapons: these could be mud, if the battle has by now reached the open air, which is not certain, or perhaps spittle if we are still inside the church

Hudibras and Trilla: these two fight in the first book of Samuel Butler's poem *Hudibras*

nymphs and swains: a neo-classical and 'pastoral' way of referring to young women and men

pattins: (or pattens) wooden over-shoes, something like clogs

Don Quixote: the hero of the satirical novel *Don Quixote* by Miguel de Cervantes

pillion: double saddle, seating two riders one behind the other

---

Book 4 Chapter 9

The Seagrims, not a peaceful family, discuss Sophia's offer to make Molly her maid. Notice the west-country dialect of the Seagrims. Among other characteristics, note the substitution of 'v' for 'f' as in 'Voke' (for 'folk'). Notice also Mrs Seagrim's mistakes ('potion' for 'portion'—(marriage settlement)—and 'gownd' for 'gown').

NOTES AND GLOSSARY:

panacea: remedy

thof':   dialect for 'though'. ('Cough', for instance, is pronounced 'koff')

marry come up: a meaningless expression denoting something like 'indeed'

Mr Freke: see note to Book 2 Chapter 4

Book 4 Chapter 10

Squire Western's curate tells him of Molly's condition; Tom leaves the table and Sophia is distressed.

Notice Squire Western's dialect. When he is excited or angry he tends to slip into broad Somerset although he is often surprisingly well-spoken.

NOTES AND GLOSSARY:

battery: here, artillery, guns

baronet ... sirloin: by tradition the cut of beef known as the sirloin was so named by King James I who so liked it that he knighted it (Sir Loin). The curate takes the joke a little further and calls the beef a baronet (a hereditary rank, higher than a knight but still carrying the title 'Sir')

Her mittimus to Bridewel: her commital to prison

malapert: awkward; out of season

libation: originally, in classical times, a libation was wine poured from the cup on to the floor with a view to placating one of the gods. Here the word is used for wine poured down the drinkers' throats

---

Book 4 Chapter 11

Tom admits that he is the father of Molly's child and thus saves her from Bridewell. Allworthy lectures him on incontinence and we hear Thwackum and Square on this subject.

Notice that Mr Allworthy is here expressly cleared of the charge of having behaved loosely with women as Western asserts. Western's 'rhodomontade' (exaggeration) is dismissed as a lie ('a much shorter word').

NOTES AND GLOSSARY:

chaice: (or chace) chase, hunt

constable: the regular police force was not, of course, formed until the mid-nineteenth century. This 'constable' is a parish officer

'in foro conscientiae': (*Latin*) in the tribunal of the conscience

mittimus: paper committing the accused to prison

gall: bitterness

Sir Richard Steele: (1672–1729) principal contributor to *The Spectator* (with Joseph Addison; see note on him, p.6) and other journals

quadrate with: square with, conform to

Book 4 Chapter 12

Sophia in and out of love with Tom. Notice Mrs Honour's speech. Once again Fielding is satirising a character and a social type (gossipy servants) through their manner of speaking. Mrs Honour talks a lot, using long sentences sometimes, and clearly-marked clauses always, to give the impression of a limited mind moving from point to point as different features of the topic catch its attention.

NOTES AND GLOSSARY:

trumpery: here, loose women
draggle-tails: sordid sluts
baggages: here, an insulting way of referring to women
whipped at the cart's tail: as prostitutes were; the cart moved through the streets to make an exhibition of the punishment
Stoic philosophy: an ancient Greek philosophy recommending, among other things, indifference to suffering

Book 4 Chapter 13

Tom's bravery; he saves Sophia from a fall and breaks his arm.

NOTES AND GLOSSARY:

Mr Osborne: Francis Osborne (1593–1659), a misogynist, wrote *Advice to a Son* (1656–8) in which the son is advised to beware of women
Mr Bayle: Pierre Bayle (1647—1706), a French Rationalist philosopher whose *Dictionary* had appeared in an English translation in 1734-7
Helen: Helen of Troy; archetype of woman in several ways: of beauty, of perfidy and (as here) of daring
Odyssey: the 'heroine' is, of course, Penelope, who waits for the return of Ulysses for twenty years, during which she is constant to him

Book 4 Chapter 14

Sophia and Tom are attended by a surgeon. Mrs Honour tells Sophia that Tom has shown signs of love.

NOTES AND GLOSSARY:

hartshorn: an ammonia-based restorative, like smelling salts
blooded: from eighteenth-century literature it would appear that the pointless practice of removing large amounts of a patient's blood (here small amounts as becomes Sophia's modesty) was almost the only treatment offered by medical practitioners to the suffering
like Patience on a monument: Shakespeare: *Twelfth Night*, II.4
magnimity: an example of Mrs Honour's mispronunciation (malapropism). The word intended is 'magnanimity'
muff: fur hand-warmer

Horace:	see General glossary. The 'rule' is to leave out what will spoil the final production. Horace, *Ars Poetica*, 149

Book 5 Chapter 1

This is an essay on the 'initial essays' that open each book. They are intended as a dull contrast to the action of the other chapters. Notice Fielding's low opinion of critics. Notice also his discussion (in the second paragraph of this chapter particularly) of the classical theory of dramatic unity. See the section on Fielding's debt to the classics in Part 3, Commentary.

NOTES AND GLOSSARY:

'cuicunque . . .':	(*Latin*) whoever is an expert in his own field must be believed
'ipse dixit':	(*Latin*) just because he says so
Horace . . . Homer:	see General glossary
Oldmixon:	a hack writer of no great merit
Pope:	see General glossary

Book 5 Chapter 2

Allworthy, Thwackum, Square, Western and Sophia visit Tom, who discovers Sophia's love for him.

NOTES AND GLOSSARY:

visitation:	here, affliction
reprobacy:	here, sin
'liberavi . . .':	(*Latin*) I have said my piece
Tully:	Marcus Tullius Cicero (106–143BC). One of his *Tusculan Questions* is 'Is Pain an Evil?'
Shaftesbury:	third Earl of Shaftesbury (1671–1713). His *Characteristics* of 1711 influenced Fielding (see Commentary p.98)
Solomon:	it is not clear which of Solomon's sayings Fielding has in mind here. (Mutter suggests St Paul's 'Evil communications corrupt good manners' from the Bible, 1 Corinthians XV:33)
quack:	false doctor offering useless medicine
nostrum:	medicine, generally fraudulent
panacea:	alleviator of all evils
Hollow:	'Halloo', 'Hello'; a hunting cry
nicest:	see General glossary

D–n, if the parson ... flick: Dammit, if the parson hadn't been in priest's clothes, I should have hit him

---

Book 5 Chapter 3

Tom realises that he loves Sophia, but he sees too many obstacles in that direction and feels, anyway, committed to Molly.

NOTES AND GLOSSARY:
opiate:	tranquillising drug
sanguine:	hopeful
coxcomb:	impertinent and foolish young rake

Book 5 Chapter 4

Mrs Honour (and the muff) reveals to Tom how much he is in love and the degree to which this is requited.

NOTES AND GLOSSARY:
Socrates:	famous Greek philosopher (469–339BC)
Bid him beat abroad . . .:	here, as elsewhere, Squire Western uses the jargon of the sportsman; in this case his metaphors are taken from shooting and the implication is that he recommends Tom not to poach on his (Western's) land. The irony is that the object of Tom's attention is not Western's servant merely, but his daughter
Troy:	a reference to the Trojan war from Virgil (*Aeneid*, II, 196). A typical classical reference by Fielding

---

Book 5 Chapter 5

Square is discovered in Molly Seagrim's bedroom. Tom is freed from his obligations towards her.

Notice the theatrical handling of this scene, which could be put on to the stage almost unchanged; note that Fielding does not let the reader in on the secret of Square's presence any more than a theatre audience would know that he was there. See the section on *Tom Jones* and the theatre in the Commentary, pp.103–4, below.

NOTES AND GLOSSARY:
amour:	here, love affair
Delta:	the fourth letter of the Greek alphabet; the capital version is written thus: Δ. The Seagrims' cottage is small, Molly's bedroom more or less an attic

booty: the spoils of crime

Like Mr Constant in the play: the reference is to Vanbrugh's play *The Provok'd Wife* (1697)

horns: the sign of cuckoldry (worn on the head by a man with an unfaithful wife)

arras: wall-hanging. In fact this is a facetious comparison between Square behind the blanket and various people behind arrases in Shakespearean and Renaissance drama, most famously Polonius in Shakespeare's *Hamlet*, III.4

Kalon: (*Greek*) the ideal good; the perfect

Nostrum: see General glossary

Book 5 Chapter 6

Tom and Sophia meet unexpectedly in the garden.

NOTES AND GLOSSARY:

ensign: the most junior rank in the army (now obsolete)

attorney: lawyer

His heart was now . . . entirely evacuated: a military metaphor; Tom's heart is no longer garrisoned by Molly, and Sophia can take possession

knave: villain

Free Masons: see note to Book 2 Chapter 4

Spartan: in Plutarch's *Lycurgus* (xviii, 1) we read of a Spartan boy who allowed a fox, which he had stolen and which he was concealing under his cloak, to tear out his stomach rather than reveal his theft. The Spartans were renowned for their toughness

hartshorn: see General glossary

Book 5 Chapter 7

Mr Allworthy makes a deathbed speech and reveals his will.

NOTES AND GLOSSARY:

the Aesculapian art: Aesculapius was the Greek god of medicine

distemper: disease (also a disturbance of the mind)

Doctor Misaubin: a French quack doctor of the period, often satirised by Fielding. Note his French accent in 'Bygar . . .' (that is, 'By God')

Cato: the lines are from Addison's tragedy *Cato* (1713)

blubbering: crying in an unmanly way

One of the Roman poets: Horace, *Epistles* II, II, 24
Albeit unused to the melting mood: this and the reference to Mrs Wilkins's
'pearls' are taken from Shakespeare's *Othello*, V.2

Book 5 Chapter 8

Mrs Wilkins, Thwackum and Square react selfishly to their legacies
from Mr Allworthy.

NOTES AND GLOSSARY:
i-fackins!: Mrs Wilkins's slang version of 'I-faith' ('In faith')
curmudgeon: mean old fellow
huddling: squashing together
arrow a servant: any servant at all
St Paul: presumably in his *Epistles*
Scripture: the Bible
deists: see note to Book 4 Chapter 4
Ovid: see General glossary

Book 5 Chapter 9

Tom reacts to Mr Allworthy's recovery. He nearly fights with Blifil.
  Notice the paragraphs starting 'To say truth . . .'. Fielding takes
many such opportunities to moralise and generalise.

NOTES AND GLOSSARY:
thorough bass: a bass part that runs throughout a piece of music
throwing in the bark: administering a medicine made from tree-bark
                (quinine)

Book 5 Chapter 10

Tom takes a walk, thinks of Sophia but meets Molly, with whom he
starts a 'parly'—and something more.

NOTES AND GLOSSARY:
Ovid: see General glossary
Circassian: the inhabitants of Circassia in the Caucasus were
                noted for their beauty, and were thus in demand for
                harems and as slaves
Grand Signior's seraglio: the harem of the Ottoman Sultan
shift: a simple dress; the word can also be used of a
                nightdress
parly: parley, talk

Aristotle:	see General glossary
Pittacus:	(651–569BC?), the ruler of Mytilene, and a law-giver
Dido:	Queen of Carthage, lover of Aeneas in Virgil's *Aeneid.* Blifil's name has been substituted for that of Dido. The meaning is 'Blifil and the divine leader arrive at the same cave'
found sitting:	caught on the ground (used, for example, of a pheasant)

Book 5 Chapter 11

Tom fights Blifil and Thwackum to defend Molly's honour and he wins the day with Western's help.

NOTES AND GLOSSARY:
This chapter is related in the epic style, opening with an epic simile and treating the conflict rather as Homer or Virgil would.

Mr Pope's period of a mile:	in his *Imitations of Donne*, Satire iv, 72, Pope accuses Bishop Hoadly of speaking or writing in 'periods' (or 'sentences') 'of a mile'. He was extremely verbose
rutting:	the mating of deer
ferine kind:	wild animals
Venus Ferina:	the goddess of the love-making of wild beasts
Samean mysteries:	sexual ceremonies on the island of Samos, where a cult of Hera existed
'genus omne . . .':	(*Latin*) the whole race of living creatures

Book 5 Chapter 12

Sophia faints, Tom helps her to recover; the whole party proceeds homewards.
    Squire Western's dialect is comprehensible enough in the context. 'Att' means 'art' as in 'Thou art.'

NOTES AND GLOSSARY:

King Porus:	an Indian monarch beaten and captured in battle by Alexander the Great in 326BC
hartshorn:	see General glossary
Arcadia:	although a real area in Greece, this country is more important for its legendary status as a pastoral paradise
smart:	here, pain from wounds

Mr Bayes's troops: in *The Rehearsal*, a play of 1671, Bayes says that he will get his dead soldiers off the stage in the same way as he got them on to it, by walking

liquorish: full of liquor, but also fun-loving, gay

those numbers which we are every day losing in the war: the War of the Austrian Succession (1740-8)

Soho! puss is not far off ... form ... stole away: once again, Western uses sporting terms. Here they are taken from beagling or working with harriers (chasing hares). 'Soho!' is a general cry to attract attention; 'puss' is the hare who has been lying in her 'form', and so on

Book 6 Chapter 1

This chapter is in the form of an essay on love.

NOTES AND GLOSSARY:

the late Dr Swift: Jonathan Swift, the great satirist, died in 1745

jakes: lavatory (the 'finders of gold' were in fact men who cleaned lavatories in common parlance)

'put the world in our own person': see Shakespeare, *Much Ado about Nothing*, II.1.216

exemplification: notice that Fielding here explicitly states it to be his aim to 'exemplify' moral truths

a man born blind: perhaps another reference to Locke (see the note to Book 4 Chapter 1)

Book 6 Chapter 2

Mrs Western, Squire Western's sister, tells the squire that she believes Sophia to be in love with Blifil. He is pleased.

NOTES AND GLOSSARY:

'Mrs' Western: although unmarried, her age entitles her to this name

a candidate in the country interest: eighteenth-century politics may seem strange to us at times; Squire Western, as we shall see, is a Jacobite, and perhaps thus a Tory, but Fielding does not put either of these first in his description of the Squire's political affiliations. Instead we hear of him as being in the agricultural interest and, generally, he is against the town and the court as well as being against the (Whig?) aristocrats and the Hanoverian monarchy. See the section on politics in the Commentary, pp.98-100

Rapin . . . Eachard: Fielding is referring to relatively recent historical works by Paul de Rapin (1661-1725) and Lawrence Eachard (1670-1730). Here, as elsewhere, there is a slight lack of English patriotism evident in Mrs Western's tastes

amour: here, the reference is to gallantry and love-making in general

Beau-monde: polite society

gibberish: nonsense

lingo: jargon; slang

'London Evening-Post': a leading anti-government paper of the day. Squire Western's sympathies are made a little clearer by this reference

A courtier . . . Presbyterian . . . Hanoverian: see the section on politics in the Commentary, pp.98-100

Lent thee a flick: hit slightly, whipped

made a shift to: somehow managed to

'fore George!: an oath derived from 'Before St George' or 'By George'

bate: abate, reduce

King Alcinous: King of the Phaeacians, who suggests that Ulysses might like to marry his daughter Nausicaa (see *Odyssey*, Book VII)

plenipo: plenipotentiary (having full powers; used of ambassadors)

Machiavel: Niccolo Machiavelli (1469-1527), an Italian political theorist associated with unscrupulous use of power

Exchange-alley: a forerunner of the modern Stock Exchange in London

Croat: Croatian (meaning, here, barbarian)

the Empress Queen: Maria Theresa (1717-80), Empress of the Holy Roman Empire

leagues: treaties

Book 6 Chapter 3

Squire Western proposes to Allworthy that Sophia and Blifil should marry. Allworthy reacts.

Fielding makes a point of Mr Allworthy's unemotional reaction to Squire Western's proposal. Tom, for instance, is far more emotional in his reactions; which of the two is really 'allworthy'?

From 'To say the truth' onwards, this chapter is a digression on wisdom.

NOTES AND GLOSSARY:

staggered:	see General glossary
rally:	here, to tease
Grosvenor Square:	a square in Mayfair, the smartest part of London
Wiltshire:	a county in south-west England
Brentford:	now a suburb of London
gamester:	gambler
countermine:	to take action against an opponent (a metaphor taken from siege warfare)
bubble:	dupe; one who is tricked by cheats
encomium:	speech of praise
elogiums:	eulogies, speeches of praise
Mr Hogarth's poor poet:	see the painting by Hogarth called *The Distressed Poet*, which shows a writer in extreme poverty
popish:	Roman Catholic

Book 6 Chapter 4

Allworthy and Western decide to bring Sophia and Blifil together.

Notice that Blifil, unlike Tom, is a very cold fish sexually; and that Allworthy 'had possessed much fire in his youth'. Similarly, Western, although even more impercipient than Allworthy, has a 'natural impetuosity' which is a great redeeming feature.

NOTES AND GLOSSARY:

tincture:	touch, the smallest amount
'Gazette':	the official paper giving diplomatic, military and other governmental information; in full, *The London Gazette*

Book 6 Chapter 5

Mrs Western and Sophia, discussing love, discover that they are mis-understanding one another and that Sophia is thinking of Jones, not Blifil. Her aunt becomes angry.

NOTES AND GLOSSARY:

book:	Sophia's book may be *David Simple*, a novel published in 1744 by Sarah, Fielding's sister
discovering:	revealing
as the French are with our motions:	that is, the French have an efficient spy-system in the current war
base-born:	of low parentage

Book 6 Chapter 6

Mrs Honour and Sophia talk, the former so much that the latter misses a chance of seeing Tom.

NOTES AND GLOSSARY:

vociferation:	raising of voices
O Gemini:	an oath, probably a more acceptable version of 'O Jesus'
preamble:	Mrs Honour's malapropism, though which word she really intends is hard to say
i-fackins!:	see note to Book 5 Chapter 8

Book 6 Chapter 7

Blifil comes to court Sophia. Mr Western threatens to disinherit Sophia if she does not marry Blifil.

The theme of paternal forcing of the daughter's hand in marriage had been very thoroughly treated in Richardson's contemporaneous novel *Clarissa* (1748).

NOTES AND GLOSSARY:

Misfortunes do not come single: among other sources of this sentiment we can include Shakespeare's 'When sorrows come, they come not single spies/But in battalions' (*Hamlet*, IV.5)

Book 6 Chapter 8 ·

Tom and Sophia meet, and talk together in great unhappiness.

NOTES AND GLOSSARY:
Racks or wheels: instruments of torture

Book 6 Chapter 9

Western is told of Sophia's passion for Tom and bursts in on them. Sophia faints and Tom leaves the house.

Notice the epic similes offered in the seventh and eighth paragraphs of this chapter.

NOTES AND GLOSSARY:

Dowdy: a practical joker who used to frighten guests in a Salisbury hotel by dressing up as a ghost

I'll lick thee:	I'll beat you in a fight
a—:	arse
the antients:	classical authors
Seneca:	Lucius Annaeus Seneca (*d*.AD65), Roman philosopher
Alexander and Clytus:	Clytus saved Alexander the Great's life but was later killed by him when drunk

Book 6 Chapter 10

Western tells Allworthy what he has discovered about Sophia and Tom. Blifil adds his own version of Tom's behaviour during Allworthy's illness.

Notice Western's dialect in this chapter. It is hardly necessary to gloss every detail of it but it is worth noting Western's dislike of 'the zinking fund' (sinking fund, a governmental reserve fund for emergencies) and of Hanover, whence came the Royal Family who had ousted the Stewarts. See the section on eighteenth-century politics in the Commentary, pp.98–100.

Fielding says of Allworthy that he 'perfectly well knew mankind'. This is doubtful; after all, he is about to misjudge Tom quite horribly.

NOTES AND GLOSSARY:

gelding's plate:	a horse-race reserved to geldings, castrated stallions
discover:	see General glossary

Book 6 Chapter 11

Mr Allworthy, quite misjudging the matter, banishes Tom 'for ever' from Paradise Hall.

'The neighbourhood' condemns Allworthy's action as cruel. Often in Fielding the mass of people are wrong, but not here, although the last sentence of the chapter shows that they are exaggerating the case.

Book 6 Chapter 12

Tom leaves home, writes to Sophia, loses five hundred pounds, and receives Sophia's reply.

NOTES AND GLOSSARY:

Lee:	Nathaniel Lee (1653–92), dramatist
wafer:	seal of a letter
to lay wires for hares:	to set traps
billet:	here, note, 'billet-doux'

Book 6 Chapter 13

Sophia receives Tom's note, is imprisoned by her father, but manages to send Tom money.

Notice how Fielding describes, in the last two paragraphs of this chapter, the (imperfect) workings of Black George's conscience.

NOTES AND GLOSSARY:
avocation: here, distraction, diversion
such a perfidy man: such a perfidious man
Marry . . .: Mrs Honour's mild oaths have some meaning perhaps. Thus 'marry' may be a corruption of 'Mary' ('Our Lady!')
arrow: here, any

Book 6 Chapter 14

Mrs Western argues with Squire Western about his treatment of Sophia, and she is let out of her prison.

NOTES AND GLOSSARY:
confide in me: have confidence in me
Milton: John Milton (1608-74), the puritan poet, author of *Paradise Lost*
Hanover Rats . . .: see the section on politics, Commentary pp.98-100

Book 7 Chapter 1

Fielding compares the world to a theatre audience, as well as to the actors in a theatre.

NOTES AND GLOSSARY:
Thespis: 'the father of Greek tragedy'; a perhaps mythical tragedian of the sixth century BC
Hissing and buffeting: showing disapproval
personating: impersonating
The hypocrite may be said to be a player . . .: the Greek word for 'actor' is the root for our word 'hypocrite'. This point of Fielding's can perhaps be used as a key to his moral concerns: Blifil, for instance, is a good *actor* (at least a good enough one to delude Allworthy) and the novelist is always showing him in situations in which the reader, with a little effort, can see through to the real character underneath

Shakespeare: the quotation is from *Macbeth*, V.1
A poem called the Deity: Samuel Boyse's poem (published 1739)
Those who sat in the world's upper gallery . . .: theatres in the eighteenth century (as later) were divided into upper gallery (nowadays 'upper circle'; 'the gods'), first gallery ('circle'; 'dress circle'), the pit ('stalls') and boxes. Price, and elegance, went in the reverse of the order listed, with the boxes being the most expensive and smartest part of the theatre
Garrick: David Garrick (1717–79), the great actor and a close friend of Fielding
Scipio the Great: Scipio Africanus Major, a Roman general (236–183BC)
Laelius the Wise: Roman orator, renowned for his friendship with the younger Scipio
Horace . . . Cicero: see General glossary
Reason the Patentee: the patentee of a theatre in the eighteenth century was the equivalent of a licensee: one permitted to perform plays by government licence
Iago: the villain in Shakespeare's *Othello*
Mr William Mills: an actor; a friend of Fielding

Book 7 Chapter 2

Tom resolves to go to sea.

NOTES AND GLOSSARY:
Milton: Fielding here specifically likens Tom to (Milton's) Adam. Tom is an 'Everyman', man in his natural goodness of heart, but man fallen into natural error. The line from Milton comes at the end of the last book of *Paradise Lost* (Book 12 line 646) and the implication is that Tom, like Adam, will now have to wander the earth until he can again find Paradise

---

Book 7 Chapter 3

Sophia tells Mrs Western that she will not marry Blifil. Squire Western bursts in and has a violent quarrel with his sister, who leaves home.

NOTES AND GLOSSARY:
Socrates . . . Alcibiades: we know little of Alcibiades' philosophy (the point is, in fact, that he had none and that Mrs

Western is mistaken), and of Socrates' philosophy the very last thing that could be said is that it is not concerned with the opinion of others. The passage establishes Mrs Western's ignorance

Bailey's Dictionary: the principal English dictionary from its publication in 1730 to the publication of Dr Samuel Johnson's dictionary in 1755

Bumtrap: a slang term for a bailiff (an early form of police officer whose business it was to obtain money from debtors by seizing their possessions)

D-n me then if shatunt ha'un: Squire Western's dialect becomes more pronounced when he is in a rage. This sentence means 'Damn me, then, if you won't have him'. 'Shatunt' is his version of 'shall not'

Plato: see General glossary

Gothic: here Mrs Western simply means 'barbarian' or 'medieval'

'boor'... 'Boar'...: this hints at Squire Western's pronunciation

Your Hanover breed...: another of the Squire's digs at the Hanoverian dynasty then on the throne

eat up: here the word 'eat' (pronounced 'et') is the past participle, 'ate'

Book 7 Chapter 4

Squire Western's relationship with his deceased wife is described. He became wildly jealous because Sophia loved her mother better than himself.

NOTES AND GLOSSARY:

his holla ...: in the first paragraph Squire Western employs an extensive range of hunting metaphors. The general idea is clear enough: he bids defiance to women in their attempts to control him

the King over the Water: the Jacobite toast: the Stuart pretenders to the British throne were, of course, living across the Channel in France

the squire's estate ....: Squire Western, in spite of his homeliness, is in fact a rich man and a great landowner. So, of course, is Allworthy. This is to be borne in mind when trying to understand the significance of Sophia's marriage: as an only child she is a highly valuable property

a bad scenting day: a bad day for hunting

vented his spleen: let out his anger
to chew the cud upon it: to think about it

Book 7 Chapter 5

Sophia and her father talk; she prevails on him to recall Mrs Western.

NOTES AND GLOSSARY:
Presbyterian Hannoverian b–: the Squire is, of course, merely looking for any insult to heap on his sister, but the implication here is that she is a 'bitch' with whose religion and politics he does not agree. The Presbyterians are low-Church Protestants, Calvinist and anti-episcopal, who would be particularly unsympathetic to the high-Church Jacobitism of Western. To Fielding's broad and generous spirit Presbyterians, like Methodists, would have seemed narrow, dismal and hypocritical Puritans; the Church of Scotland, incidentally, (the 'Kirk') is a good example of a Presbyterian sect
She may 'dite me of a plot: she may 'accuse me' ('indict me') of being a Jacobite. Some leading Jacobites lost their estates after the abortive rebellions of 1715 and 1745
the College of Chambermaids: Fielding jokingly suggests a parallel between the remedies of servants for love-sick mistresses and the remedies of such bodies as the College of Surgeons

---

Book 7 Chapter 6

Because of the Squire's impatience (and Blifil's cunning) Sophia's wedding is hastened forward.

NOTES AND GLOSSARY:
Horace: see General glossary
Follow her . . .: once again Western indulges in rather offensive hunting terms to encourage Blifil (who is not a sportsman, naturally) to marry Sophia
Popish inquisitor . . . lay power: Fielding refers to the Inquisition and its relationship with the civil ('lay') government
Tho' Mr Blifil was not of the complexion of Jones . . .: 'complexion' here means 'nature'. Blifil's appetite for Sophia is made to sound slightly disgusting (she is an 'ortolan', a delicacy of the table) and it is certainly perverse (he

likes the fact that she hates him) and even perverted (he wishes to humiliate her in revenge for her aversion to him). This paragraph, and the next two, demonstrate Fielding's immense care and accuracy in presenting moral characters and situations

Salvo: salve, soothing ointment

Book 7 Chapter 7

Sophia resolves to run away from home.

Notice that Mrs Honour seems to talk, at times, in the voice of religion but in fact recommends selfishness.

NOTES AND GLOSSARY:
O lud, ma'am: Oh Lord, madam; an expression of surprise and, here, horror
One had lieverer: One had rather

Book 7 Chapter 8

Mrs Honour decides to go with Sophia; she finds a way of bringing about her dismissal.

NOTES AND GLOSSARY:
Quivedo: Francisco Gomez de Quevedo (1580–1645), Spanish satirist and writer of picaresque fiction
a glouting humour: gloomy, in a bad temper
trumpery . . . audacious saucy trollop . . . hussy . . .: once again the servants have a string of insulting terms (all meaning something like 'loose woman') to trade with each other

Book 7 Chapter 9

Mrs Honour is sent away and Sophia arranges to meet her.

NOTES AND GLOSSARY:
Bridewell: see General glossary
Justice . . . clerk: from the sixteenth century until the present day the first level of justice in England has been administered by magistrates, or JPs (Justices of the Peace). For serious crimes they must pass the accused person on to higher courts but they deal with a wide range of minor matters. In the eighteenth century

they were the backbone of local law-enforcement and, as they were usually landowners, they tended to be most enthusiastic about enforcing the fierce laws against poaching. Then, as now, most Justices of the Peace were amateurs and often depended on their professional clerks to advise them as to the law. Squire Western is not the most scrupulous of justices and he has had two complaints made against him in the High Court in London ('he had already had two informations exhibited against him in the King's-Bench')

that strange prodigious creature man: this is a quotation from the satirist Lord Rochester. His *Satyr Against Mankind* (1679) is an early example of the tradition of satire that runs from Samuel Butler's *Hudibras* of the 1660s through Rochester, Dryden, Swift and Pope to Fielding himself

a certain little passion . . . : here, Fielding attributes to Sophia her only moment of vice: the 'passion' is pride, of course, in its bad sense

Cupid: the classical god of love

Punchinello: Punch in the 'Punch and Judy' puppet show

Book 7 Chapter 10

Tom meets a hypocritical Quaker, and spends the night sleeping on a chair in a low tavern.

Notice the Somerset accents of the country people Tom meets. They say 'measter' for 'master', 'thick' for 'that' and 'zuch' for 'such', rather like Squire Western.

NOTES AND GLOSSARY:

Quaker: the Quakers (properly 'The Society of Friends'— notice that the first word this Quaker says is 'Friend') are a puritan Protestant sect advocating simplicity of life, dress and manner. As Puritans they were unpopular with Fielding. He refers slightly sarcastically to their 'silent meetings' (at which there was no formal liturgy but anyone could speak if 'the spirit moved them'), to their clothing ('Broadbrim' refers to their hats) and, finally, to their being as snobbish as other men. Notice the Quaker's Biblical style of speech

Two pair of stairs: two storeys up; up four flights of stairs

Book 7 Chapter 11

A company of soldiers arrives at the tavern. Tom volunteers to join them.

NOTES AND GLOSSARY:

Gentlemen in red coats:	throughout the eighteenth and nineteenth centuries the characteristic uniform of the British Army was bright red
the last trumpet:	supposedly, the trumpet which will blow at the end of the world to wake the dead
extenuate:	here, make less
the rebels ... the Duke of Cumberland ... the late rebellion ...:	here we begin to learn the historical setting of the novel. Fielding took great care with the chronology and mechanics of his story, deliberately synchronising it with the 1745 rebellion (the novel was written between 1746 and 1748), led by Bonnie Prince Charlie and finally put down by 'Butcher' Cumberland at Culloden. Bonnie Prince Charlie was supported by a number of Scots chiefs, lairds and and gentry but his invasion of England did not provoke the Jacobite gentry (such as Squire Western, presumably) into joining him in large numbers, and the rebellion failed. Fielding was ardently anti-Jacobite and edited several newspapers which defended the Hanoverian settlement. See the section on eighteenth-century politics in the Commentary, pp.98–100
gauntlope:	gauntlet; large glove
glisters:	glistens
halberd:	a weapon denoting the sergeant's rank

Book 7 Chapter 12

Tom dines with the officers of his new company. His toast to Sophia provokes a brawl during which he is knocked unconscious.

Notice the irony of a Frenchman being a lieutenant in the British Army. Fielding manages to convey his French accent and halting English rather well.

NOTES AND GLOSSARY:

Tannieres:	part of Marlborough's campaign against the French of 1709

Ensign:	this rank, which no longer exists, was the most junior rank of officer in some regiments
Pope's Homer:	see General glossary
Madame Daciere:	(1654–1720) translator of Homer into French
Corderius:	(1479–1564), a Renaissance writer in Latin, whose work Northerton has been made to study at school
put:	here, fool
the devil a smack:	none at all
nick:	here, outwit
cull:	here, dupe, fool,
pimp:	here, hypocrite
smoke:	here, tease, show up, notice the faults of
discharged a bottle:	Northerton throws the whole bottle at Tom; he does not merely empty it over him
drawer:	here, drawer of beer, a waiter
the physical order:	doctors
bleeding:	almost the only cure ever used for anything in eighteenth-century fiction seems to be the (dangerous and pointless) practice of removing blood from the patient

---

Book 7 Chapter 13

Tom seems more ill than he really is. A duel is threatened.

Notice the landlady's accent. Particularly she pronounces 'thought' as 'thoft' and 'ought' as 'oft'. She also, perhaps affecting a higher class than she belongs to, says 'sartain' for 'certain' and 'parson' for 'person'.

Notice also the prolix and jargon-ridden talk of the doctor. As the point here is that his audience cannot understand all that he says, and indeed he may not understand it all himself, there is no need for the reader to grasp more than the general idea that he is concealing his ignorance under a barrage of nonsense.

Notice the discussion, in the latter part of this chapter, of honour. See General glossary.

NOTES AND GLOSSARY:

sack-whey ... water gruel:	respectively, an attractive and an unappetising concoction
buss:	kiss

Book 7 Chapter 14

Tom gets up and tries to find Northerton in order to fight with him, but he has disappeared.

Notice Tom's dilemma between his Christian duty not to seek revenge and his manly duty to uphold his honour.

NOTES AND GLOSSARY:
bolster: pillow
a vociferous drawer: a noisy servant
halberdier: sergeant
battle of Dettingen: fought in 1743 in the war of the Austrian Succession
twenty guineas: twenty pounds and twenty shillings (in fact, therefore, twenty-one pounds). Thus twenty-one times as much as the twenty shillings mentioned later
Banquo: Banquo's ghost returns, all bloody about the head, to haunt Macbeth in Shakespeare's play (II.2)
ague: a fever, similar to malaria, common in England until the nineteenth century
antic: here, mad
the applause of the galleries: the applause of the cheaper parts of the theatre (see note on p.42)

Book 7 Chapter 15

Tom is in bed; the commotion in the inn is settled and the soldiers prepare to march away.

NOTES AND GLOSSARY:
Nemesis: see General glossary
a certain wooden edifice: the gallows
'quomodo': (*Latin*) the means
But hark, the general beats: listen, a drum beats (the drum would be calling the soldiers together for their march)

Book 8 Chapter 1

This chapter concerns the use of the 'marvellous' or supernatural in fiction and contains a plea for the 'probable', that is, realism.

NOTES AND GLOSSARY:
prolegomenous: having the nature of a preface
M. Dacier: André Dacier (1651–1722), translator of Aristotle's *Poetics*
the Phaeacians: the Greek nation to whom Ulysses recounts a large part of his adventures in the *Odyssey*
Polypheme: the Cyclops whom Ulysses outwits in the *Odyssey*, thereby avoiding being eaten by him

Circe: a witch in the *Odyssey* who changed men into pigs
Lord Shaftesbury: the third Earl of Shaftesbury (1671–1713), whose
                     book *Characteristics* influenced Fielding
'Hudibras':   Samuel Butler's satirical poem, begun in 1662
Hippocrene or Helicon: Hippocrene was a fountain on Mount Helicon
                     in Greece. Its water was supposed to bring inspira-
                     tion to poets
such was the successless armament of Xerxes . . .: this passage lists
                     remarkable defeats and victories which, although
                     true enough, test credibility
George Villiers . . . Dr Drelincourt . . . Mrs Veale: the ghost of George
                     Villiers warned his son, the Duke of Buckingham,
                     to ingratiate himself with the people and avoid
                     assassination. The warning went unheeded and the
                     duke was killed. Drelincourt wrote *The Christian's
                     Defence against the Fear of Death* (trans. into
                     English 1675). Mrs Veale is the subject of Defoe's
                     pamphlet in which life after death is vindicated and
                     shown to exist
the History of the Rebellion: the Earl of Clarendon's large work on the
                     Cromwellian period. The story of the ghost of
                     George Villiers appears in the first book of this
Trojan . . . Antonius: these were supposedly good Roman Emperors as
                     against the evil ones typified by Nero and Caligula
Hamlet: in this play Hamlet aims to 'catch the conscience of
                     the king' and make him reveal his guilt of the murder
                     of Hamlet's father. The comparison with the Fisher
                     and Derby story is not very good, but the general
                     ideas of ingratitude and bad conscience apply in
                     both cases
scrutore: desk
Suetonius: Gaius Suetonius Tranquillus (*c.*AD70–*c.*160), his-
                     torian of the first twelve Emperors of Rome
'—Quis credet? . . . nemo': (*Latin*) Who will believe it? Nobody,
                     Hercules! nobody. Perhaps one or two; perhaps
                     nobody (Fielding's version of lines from the Roman
                     poet Persius where '*credet*' is replaced by '*leget*' —
                     'who will *read* it?')
'Rarae aves':   (*Latin*) rare birds
To hitch him in a distich: to catch him in a couple of lines of poetry
Tyburn: where London's gallows stood (near where Marble
                     Arch now stands)
Bathos: the reference is to Pope's *Peri-Bathos, or: The Art
                     of Sinking in Poetry* (1728), a satire on poor poetry

Book 8 Chapter 2

Tom talks to the landlady of the inn.
Notice the landlady's appalling loquacity.

NOTES AND GLOSSARY:
narrow . . . arrow: not one . . . any
ordinary: food in a tavern from a public table (also known as 'table d'hôte')
La, my seeming: well, it seems to me . . .
Angels are painted fair . . .: Tom is quoting from Thomas Otway's play Venice Preserv'd (1682)
gratis: (originally Latin) free, without charge

Book 8 Chapter 3

The avaricious surgeon, like the landlady, turns against Tom when he discovers how poor he is.
Notice the incomprehensible medical jargon attributed to the surgeon. He too is a hypocrite—or player.

NOTES AND GLOSSARY:
animadverting on: complaining about
an arrant scrub: clearly a scoundrel

Book 8 Chapter 4

Tom meets Benjamin the barber.
Notice Benjamin's Latin. He uses a few stock phrases and well-known Latin tags again and again in all contexts. Usually they merely apply in a general way to what he is saying and therefore do not add much to, or subtract much from, his drift. Where they matter translations will be supplied in these Notes.

NOTES AND GLOSSARY:
the Barber of Bagdad: a comic character in The Arabian Nights
he in Don Quixote: the chief barber in Don Quixote is one Nicolas whose barber's basin is mistaken by the mad Quixote for the mythical Mambrino's helmet
carrying coals to Newcastle: a good proportion of the coal used in London came from the mining areas around Newcastle; the implication is that one does not take things to where there are already the same things in abundance

Adonis ... Venus: in classical mythology the goddess Venus fell in love with a beautiful mortal youth, Adonis, with disastrous consequences

'The Sun': rooms in inns and taverns had names (often those of flowers, vegetables or heavenly bodies). Gentry would always use these private rooms when visiting an inn

a poor parish boy: the poor of each parish were maintained by a local tax (Poor Relief). Bastards and beggars were among those who were unwelcome in villages in case they claimed this relief

bye-blow: side-blow, a bastard

'festina lente': (*Latin*) hasten slowly

'non omnia possumus omnes': (*Latin*) we can't all do everything

'non tanto me dignor honore': (*Latin*) I am not worthy of such an honour

'hinc illae lachrymae': (*Latin*) hence those tears

'in statu quo': (*Latin*) as it was

Book 8 Chapter 5

Tom tells the barber his identity and circumstances.

Benjamin's library seems to have a little of everything, but not very much of anything.

NOTES AND GLOSSARY:
'doctissime tonsorum': (*Latin*) most learned of barbers
'Ago tibi gratias, domine': (*Latin*) I thank you, Lord
'Proh deum atque hominum fidem!': (*Latin*) by the faith of gods and men
'ille optimus omnium patronus': (*Latin*) that best of all patrons
'casu incognito': (*Latin*) unknown causes
'Pauca verba': (*Latin*) few words
'Non si male nunc et olim sic erat': (*Latin*) if it is bad now it was not so once
'amoris abundantia erga te': (*Latin*) full of love towards you
'Tempus edax rerum': (*Latin*) time the conqueror of things

Book 8 Chapter 6

Benjamin turns out to be Partridge. He decides to accompany Tom.

NOTES AND GLOSSARY:
'tonsor': (*Latin*) barber
'ars omnibus communis': (*Latin*) the art is common to all

'**Infandum, regina . . .**': (*Latin*) you command me, queen, to speak again of a terrible sorrow
'**vis unita fortior**': (*Latin*) united strength is stronger
'**nil desperandum . . . Teucro**': (*Latin*) do not despair, Teucer is leader and protector

---

Book 8 Chapter 7

Tom and the landlady's husband become acquainted. Tom and Partridge depart.

NOTES AND GLOSSARY:
smart-money: money paid to soldiers who had received wounds
Ulysses: in Homer's *Odyssey* he spent ten years trying to get home to Ithaca after the fall of Troy
As Jones had not this gift from nature: that is, Tom, being naturally good, is not naturally suspicious

---

Book 8 Chapter 8

Tom and Partridge stop at an inn in Gloucester where Tom is again recognised and vilified.

NOTES AND GLOSSARY:
Whitefield . . . Methodism: George Whitefield (1714–70) was a founder of the Methodist (i.e. somewhat Puritan) branch of the Church of England. (In 1795 Methodists split off to form a separate Church.) He was indeed a 'great preacher' who, with the Wesley brothers, gained a great following for Methodism in Britain and America. Whitefield tended towards a more Calvinistic theology and was thus particularly distasteful to Fielding who disliked the fanaticism of Methodism and the spiritual arrogance of Calvin (see note to Book 1 Chapter 10)
a long hood . . . : the landlord's wife put on the clothing of a Methodist woman and waited for the 'Spirit' to move her. A typical gesture, according to Fielding, who was sceptical of the sudden 'conversions' recorded by Wesley's followers
attorney: solicitor, lawyer
petty-fogger: small-time lawyer, probably corrupt
Train-bearers: carriers of the ends of robes; thus unimportant ceremonial figures

hackneys of attornies: literally, 'lawyers' horses'. A hackney was an ordinary horse, as opposed to a special horse for hunting or racing

timbersome: Mrs Whitefield's malapropism for 'timorous', easily frightened

---

Book 8 Chapter 9

Tom and Partridge are on the road from Gloucester. Partridge nearly reveals that he is a Jacobite.

NOTES AND GLOSSARY:

Milton: see General glossary

'Spectator': the most famous of several journals conducted by Addison and Steele in the earlier eighteenth century

'per devia rura viarum': (*Latin*) by remote country ways

'interdum stultus opportuna loquitur': (*Latin*) sometimes a fool speaks opportunely (that is, in the right place)

Tramontane: (*from the Latin*) a barbarian from beyond the mountains

Briaraeus: a Homeric giant with a hundred hands

Hudibras: see General glossary

Virgil: see General glossary

The Pretender: Bonnie Prince Charlie, leader of the 1745 rebellion and pretender to the British throne

Ward's pill: Dr Joshua Ward (1685–1761) was a well known doctor of the day. His pill was an analgesic of no real efficacy

---

Book 8 Chapter 10

Tom and Partridge stop at the Man of the Hill's house; they rescue him from robbers and ask to hear his story.

In this chapter (and the next) the character of Partridge is established. He is cowardly and selfish but, like Sancho Panza, Don Quixote's squire, he combines these with an attractive personality. He is, at least, not malicious or grasping and is weak enough, unlike some other villains in the novel, for Tom always to be able to bully him back on to the straight and narrow path.

NOTES AND GLOSSARY:

Otway in his Orphan: Thomas Otway's tragedy of 1680

the reign of James the First: James I (1603–25) of England was a persecutor of witches

Book 8 Chapter 11

The Man of the Hill tells the first part of his story. He is interrupted by Partridge who tells something of *his* story.

Fielding is at home in the south-west of England. The Man of the Hill goes to school at Taunton, having been born in Somersetshire.

NOTES AND GLOSSARY:

Xantippe . . . Socrates:	Xantippe was the wife of Socrates; she had a reputation for abusing and bullying her husband
Black Monday:	schoolboy slang for the first day of the school year
Vice-Chancellor:	senior academic and official of a university
coxcomb:	impertinent fellow
chum:	here, university slang for a friend with whom one shares digs or rooms
forty guineas:	forty pounds and forty shillings (that is, forty-two pounds)
escritoire:	desk
chaise:	coach
cronies:	friends
paramour:	mistress
'habeas corpus':	(*Latin*) an injunction, handed out by a court, to produce a prisoner in person. In this case the *habeas corpus* is needed to get the Man of the Hill out of gaol so that he can stand trial at Oxford
Ovid's Epistles:	Francis has advanced some way in Latin if he can read several lines of Ovid's prose without a dictionary, but Ovid is not the hardest Latin writer
're' and 'cognosco':	(*Latin*) Partridge's pedantry is accurate enough but is rather compromised by his describing 'recognisance' as 'a hard word'

Book 8 Chapter 12

The Man of the Hill's story is continued.

Notice the similarity of this part of the Man of the Hill's story to the Spanish picaresque narratives of the sixteenth and seventeenth centuries to which Fielding was probably indebted: *Lazarillo de Tormes* (anon, 1553), *Guzman de Alfarache* by Mateo Aleman (1547–1614), *El Buscon* by Francisco de Quevedo (1580–1645), and others.

NOTES AND GLOSSARY:

Leadenhall Market: a meat and produce market in the City of London, still in existence

'effodiuntur . . . malorum': (*Latin*) riches, which are the provokers of
evil, have to be dug for

queer cull . . . nubbing cheat . . .: Watson uses thieves' slang. A 'queer
cull' is a dupe or gull who is penniless or otherwise
useless; the 'nubbing cheat', as Partridge learns, is
the gallows; 'running a levant' is betting and then
running away if the bet loses; a 'rum cull' is a rich
or gullible one

Book 8 Chapter 13

The Man of the Hill's story is continued.

NOTES AND GLOSSARY:
collegiate: fellow-student (here, of crime)
sharpers: tricksters; fraud-perpetrators
Aristotle and Plato: see General glossary
Horace: see General glossary

Book 8 Chapter 14

The Man of the Hill concludes his story.

NOTES AND GLOSSARY:
the Duke of Monmouth was landed in the west . . .: Monmouth, bastard
son of Charles II, in 1685 landed in the west of
England with a small force of rebels whose aim was
to oust the Catholic James II. The paragraph opening 'Events of this nature . . .' contains an argument
in favour of Monmouth, that James II's Catholicism was a danger to Anglicanism. Tom's reply to
this argument, with which he seems to agree, is
that in the present emergency (the 1745 rebellion)
where a Catholic prince is invading a Britain ruled
by a Protestant ruler, the duty of every Protestant
is clearly to rally to the Hanoverian George II (see
section on politics in the Commentary, pp.98–100)
Virgil: see General glossary
'varium et mutabile semper': (*Latin*) always changing and variable
Glorious Revolution: James II was finally deposed in 1688 and succeeded
by the Protestant William III, a Dutch prince who
had married Mary, James II's daughter, with whom
he ruled jointly (see section on politics in the
Commentary)

Book 8 Chapter 15

The Man of the Hill and Tom discuss human nature and the world.
Notice the contrast between the Man of the Hill's dislike of his
fellows and Tom's genial humanism.

NOTES AND GLOSSARY:
'valets à louage': (*French*) servants for hire
knave...fop...sloven: respectively a base-born fellow, a dandy, and an
ill-dressed lout
stews: here, brothels
jakes: lavatories
lucubrations: studies, especially those done at night

Book 9 Chapter 1

This is an essay on the authors of good novels (Fielding calls them
'histories'), and on imitating nature rather than other writers.
Notice the quality 'liberality of spirit', mentioned in this chapter.
Tom has a lot of it, Blifil none; 'men of low birth and education' are
without it, according to Fielding.

NOTES AND GLOSSARY:
'Their good brother...': an ass in Aesop's *Fables*, a collection of caution-
ary tales supposed to have been written by a Greek
slave of the sixth century BC
Rowe: Nicholas Rowe (1674–1718) edited Shakespeare
and wrote plays in imitation of his style
Horace: Horace (see General glossary) refers in his *Epistles*
to the virtue of Cato but asks whether imitation of
his style of dress by someone would indicate the
same virtue in that person
numbers: here, metre; the ability to write rhythmically
novels and romances: both of these terms were somewhat pejorative in
the eighteenth and nineteenth centuries as implying
light and valueless fictional creations
'pruritus': itch
'belles lettres': (*French*) literature
Mr Miller: Philip Miller (1691–1771), writer on gardening
Shakespeare ... Clive: besides Shakespeare himself, Fielding refers to
Ben Jonson (1572–1637), William Wycherly (1640–
1716) and Thomas Otway (1652–85), dramatists,
and David Garrick (1717–79), Mrs Cibber (1714–
66) and Mrs Clive (1711–85), actor and actresses

Those fine and nervous descriptions: 'nervous' here means 'full of the
                                energy of the human nerves'
'è converso':   (*Italian*) to turn it the other way, or 'vice-versa'

Book 9 Chapter 2

Tom rescues a woman who is being assaulted by Ensign Northerton.

NOTES AND GLOSSARY:
Aurora: dawn
'Anglicè':   (*Italian*) in English
Orpheus and Eurydice: Orpheus, in the Greek myth, was permitted to
                     rescue his wife, Eurydice, from hell on condition
                     that he did not look back at her as they walked up
                     to the daylight. But he did look, and consequently
                     lost her

Book 9 Chapter 3

The Battle of Upton. Tom, Partridge and Mrs Waters fight the person-
nel of an inn where they have been insulted.

NOTES AND GLOSSARY:
the temple of Vesta: in Rome; the temple was served by sacred virgins
Desdemona . . . Cassio: characters in Shakespeare's *Othello*
Thalestris . . . Amazons: Thalestris was supposedly the queen of the
                     female warriors, the Amazons, at the time of Alex-
                     ander the Great
the poor unfortunate Helen: Helen of Troy, married to Menelaus, King
                     of Sparta; she was abducted by Paris, the son of
                     Priam, King of Troy, and was thus the immediate
                     cause of the Trojan War

Book 9 Chapter 4

Peace is made and toasted.

NOTES AND GLOSSARY:
pillowbere: pillow-case
I defy anybody to say black is my eye: I challenge anybody to contradict
                     me
libation: ceremonial pouring out of wine in honour of the
                     gods. Here, the pouring is simply down various
                     throats

Book 9 Chapter 5

Tom and Mrs Waters dine and make love.

NOTES AND GLOSSARY:

Ulysses:	hero of Homer's *Odyssey*
Hercules:	mythical Greek hero of immense strength
Adonis:	in Greek legend, the type of masculine beauty
animal spirits:	in early medicine these are supposed to permeate the blood, giving energy
Cremona fiddle:	a violin of good quality, made in the Italian city of Cremona
Pasiphae:	in Greek mythology the mother of the Minotaur, the monster kept by King Minos of Crete

'spicula & faces amoris': (Latin) the darts and flames of love

Ovid: see General glossary

Say then, you Graces . . .: notice the invocation (here of the Graces rather than the Muses) with which Fielding prefaces his description of Tom and Mrs Waters together. Note also the hilarious mock-classical style of this love scene

'dignus vindice nodus': (*Latin*) a knot worth untying. The affair may be too trivial for the God of Eating to be concerned with. The phrase is from Horace

Dutch defence: no real defence at all

Book 9 Chapter 6

In the kitchen of the inn Tom's identity is discussed; another fight ensues.

NOTES AND GLOSSARY:

loves the cloth: here the meaning is that Mrs Waters loves soldiers; 'the cloth', however, more usually refers to the clergy. Scarlet or black is the choice

'Veritas odium parit': (*Latin*) truth begets hatred

numscull's pate: fool's head

'magisters': (*Latin*) masters

I write gentleman after my name: just as we now write 'Esq' (Esquire) after the names of people we respect (for example, 'John Brown Esq,' on the envelope of a letter) so it was once customary to write 'John Brown Gent', which implied much the same thing. (Compare 'Sir John Brown, Knight' or 'Sir John Brown, Bart'—

Baronet.) The main thing here, however, is that Partridge is laying claim to the magical status of *Gentleman*. It is hard for us to understand the importance of this distinction but it is vital to an understanding of *Tom Jones* and the whole of the eighteenth and nineteenth centuries. Gentlemen were educated (note Partridge's Latin) and were supposed not to work, being supported by their estates; they were entitled to coats of arms and the respect of others. Much of the literature of the period works in the margin between the class of 'gentry' and the next class below, the expanding middle class. Thus Tom is educated and brought up as a gentleman (he knows Latin, hunting and the birch) but the ambiguity of his birth undermines this; on the other hand he never ceases to be a gentleman just because he is short of money—even then he is intellectually and morally gentlemanly. We could see *Tom Jones* as a class novel in which a gentleman is flung out into the darkness of poverty and, potentially, the middle class or worse but who (a) remains a 'true gentleman' throughout and (b), partly for this reason, is readmitted to the 'paradise' of landowning, upper-class life at the end. His reward is Sophia—clearly a perfect lady

'Amici sumus': (*Latin*) we are friends
Schollards: scholars
running away from her friends: see 'friends' and 'family' in the General glossary

---

Book 9 Chapter 7

How Mrs Waters got into her predicament with Northerton.

NOTES AND GLOSSARY:
linnen: here, underclothes and shirts

Book 10 Chapter 1

Critics, plagiarism and the depiction of character are discussed.

NOTES AND GLOSSARY:
Sir Epicure Mammon: a gross character in Ben Jonson's *Alchemist* (1610)

Sir Fopling Flutter: the main character in George Etherege's *Man of Mode* (1676)

Sir Courtly Nice: the main character in John Crowne's *Sir Courtly Nice* (1685)

Juvenal: Decimus Junius Juvenalis (AD60–130), Roman satirist

'quas humana . . . natura': see Book 11, Chapter 1, where the complete Latin quotation, with translation, is given

Book 10 Chapter 2

Tom is caught in Mrs Water's bedroom but manages to escape censure.

Notice the Irish accents of Fitzpatrick and Maclachlan (for instance, 'maning' for 'meaning').

NOTES AND GLOSSARY:

ostler: groom

a gentleman arrived there post: that is, he arrived in great haste. It would certainly help the student of *Tom Jones* to understand the eighteenth century better if he were to look into the travelling arrangements of the period. Looking up 'post', 'inn', 'coach' and such words in the *Oxford English Dictionary* would be a good start

One of Mrs Behn's novels: Mrs Aphra Behn (1640–89), writer of novels and plays—not really a writer of 'good literature'

Book 10 Chapter 3

Sophia and Mrs Honour arrive at the inn at Upton, in disguise.

NOTES AND GLOSSARY:

Worcestershire perry: perry is like cider, but made from pears

two errant scrubs: two low fellows on their travels (unless the landlady is using 'errant' for 'arrant')

groat: four old pence

sack-whey: a light medicinal drink

habit: here, dress

mantua: a loose dress

Book 10 Chapter 4

Mrs Honour's behaviour in the inn kitchen is described. She discovers that Tom is in the house.

NOTES AND GLOSSARY:
nostrums: see General glossary
'fourberie':   (*French*) deceit
grasiers: (graziers) farm-hands, cow-men
'Non semper . . . nominativus': Partridge is showing off his Latin to one who cannot understand it; what he says is merely a grammatical rule, of no relevance here
'Quare non?':   (*Latin*) why not?

Book 10 Chapter 5

Sophia learns that Tom is in bed with Mrs Waters, and leaves the inn in indignation.

NOTES AND GLOSSARY:
never a barrel the better herring: that is, two barrels containing herrings must be much the same as all herrings are alike; so, Sophia must be as bad as Mrs Honour
'Noscitur a socio': (*Latin*) a man is known by his friends
trulls: low prostitutes
quality: a rather self-conscious way of referring to gentry
'Sbodlikins: an oath derived from a diminutive version of 'God's body'
jackanapes: fool, rogue

Book 10 Chapter 6

Tom discovers, to his great chagrin, that Sophia has been in the inn. The Irishmen prepare to leave.

NOTES AND GLOSSARY:
Blunderbuss . . . pop-gun: respectively the largest and smallest sorts of firearm. A pop-gun, of course, would be merely a child's toy
beggar all description: a reference to Cleopatra, in Shakespeare's *Antony and Cleopatra*, II.2, who 'beggar'd all description'
hit off a fault: a hunting term, meaning 'find a lost scent'—something a poor hound could not do

---

Book 10 Chapter 7

Squire Western appears at the Upton inn and confusion breaks out; everyone leaves the town in different directions.

NOTES AND GLOSSARY:
Bedlam: a famous lunatic asylum in London

Book 10 Chapter 8

This is a retrospect, in which we hear how Squire Western and Blifil discovered Sophia's escape.

NOTES AND GLOSSARY:
e'en such a man . . .: from Shakespeare's *2 Henry IV*, I.1
Hercules . . . Hylas: in Greek legend, Hercules loved Hylas, a beautiful boy, but lost him to some water-nymphs who carried him off. Hercules called for him in vain
Echo: personified as a woman in Ovid's *Metamorphoses*
Job: proverbially patient under affliction as his story in the Book of Job in the Bible makes clear
Circassian: see note to Book 5 Chapter 10
Salique Law: a law which excluded women from inheriting the throne in certain countries

---

Book 10 Chapter 9

This is a further retrospect, describing Sophia's flight. This chapter brings Sophia's story, and Squire Western's, up to the point reached in Tom's story.

NOTES AND GLOSSARY:
Arria: this Roman lady, in AD42, showed her husband how to commit suicide by stabbing herself and handing him the dagger
Anacreon: a Greek poet (563-478BC)
Hudibras: see 'Butler' in the General glossary

Book 11 Chapter 1

This chapter discusses critics, advising against slander and excessive severity.

NOTES AND GLOSSARY:
Who steals my gold . . .: this quotation from *Othello*, II.3 should read 'who steals my purse . . .'
Macduff: in Shakespeare's *Macbeth* Macduff exclaims 'Thou hast no children'
Aristotle . . . Bossu: all critics

'in foro literario':   (*Latin*) in the literary forum
Martial: Marcus Valerius Martialis (AD40–104), a Roman poet famous for his epigrams

Book 11 Chapter 2

Sophia meets her cousin Harriet, who ran away from Squire Western's five years before and is now Mrs Fitzpatrick. They are taken for Jacobite women.

Notice the discussion at the end of this chapter: there is a moral issue at stake in the question of whether to betray Sophia or not.

NOTES AND GLOSSARY:
the Severn: a major river in the west of England. Upton's full name is Upton-on-Severn
the young Chevalier . . . the Duke's army: Bonnie Prince Charlie was known as 'the Chevalier', a term perhaps adopted to avoid giving offence in conversation as it neither claimed him as king nor condemned him as a pretender. 'The Duke' is his opponent, the Duke of Cumberland
to tap away directly: to march off at a brisk pace (here, presumably to join the rebels)
Madam Jenny Cameron herself: supposedly, but not actually, the Chevalier's mistress

Book 11 Chapter 3

Sophia and Harriet together. They decide to spend the night at the inn.

Notice the skill with which Fielding interweaves the historical background of this novel (the 1745 rebellion) with the plot he is constructing with his characters.

Book 11 Chapter 4

Mrs Fitzpatrick's story is told.

NOTES AND GLOSSARY:
Machiavels: Machiavellis, devious and cunning people, so called because of Niccolò Machiavelli (1469–1527) a Florentine political theorist with a sinister public image
the Pump: one of the watering-places at Bath, the popular spa of Georgian England

Mr Nash:	Richard 'Beau' Nash (1674–1762), Master of Ceremonies at Bath, renowned for his elegance of dress and manner; he exerted a civilising effect on the town's social life and made it a fashionable resort

Book 11 Chapter 5

Mrs Fitzpatrick's story is continued.

NOTES AND GLOSSARY:

the Rooms:	the Assembly Rooms, the smart place of resort at Bath
coeval:	of the same age
Chamont . . . 'Orphan':	Thomas Otway's tragedy of 1680. Chamont is a soldier, honest but rough and insensitive

Book 11 Chapter 6

Sophia is thrown into a fright by the landlord who says that he 'knows' her; in fact he takes her for Jenny Cameron.

Notice the hints given by the landlord in the paragraph that opens 'Our landlord thought . . .'. 'All may end better than anybody expects' refers to the hopes of the Jacobites; 'some folks who have given other folks the slip' refers to the Chevalier's Scottish army by-passing the English army in its march south; London was the aim of the rebels. All these hints are, of course, given a very different interpretation by Sophia.

Book 11 Chapter 7

Mrs Fitzpatrick's story is concluded.

Notice Mrs Fitzpatrick's reading. These volumes do not indicate any particular bent in the lady's mind, nor do they seem to have a satirical purpose, being serious works by writers of history, philosophy, church polemics, and verse as well as novels.

NOTES AND GLOSSARY:

had I been possessed of the Indies . . .:	had I been rich. As a source of gold the lands of the east were accounted wealthy

Book 11 Chapter 8

Mrs Honour attacks the landlord for suggesting that Sophia is the 'whore', Jenny Cameron. The Irish peer who helped Mrs Fitzpatrick escape from her husband arrives.

Notice the references to Cervantes's *Don Quixote* in the paragraph opening 'Sophia was very soon eased . . .'. *Don Quixote*, well known to Fielding, was in fact a satire on the novels of chivalry, such as *Amadis of Gaul* (based on a variety of originals from the twelfth to the fourteenth centuries; it was translated into French in 1540), that were so popular in sixteenth-century Europe. Typically these involved the exploits of a knight errant who, among other things, would rescue 'imprisoned nymphs' in spite of the efforts of 'enchanters'—wizards or magicians.

NOTES AND GLOSSARY:

that gate, which seems to derive . . . : Fielding is referring to Billingsgate, the fish-market of London. The name could, with imagination, be derived from 'bi' and 'linguas', 'two-tongued', or 'with two languages'. The fish-porters and oyster-wenches, here compared with Virgilian nymphs (Naiades), were well known for their loud and vulgar speech. No doubt they were often influenced in this by drinking gin ('the rich distillation from the juniper berry') and whisky ('malt')

Jenny Cameron . . . The Pretender: see the section on politics in Part 3, Commentary

'Hinc illae lachrymae': (*Latin*) hence those tears

Nell Gwynn: (1650–87), mistress of Charles II

Dr Cheney: a vegetarian, properly 'Cheyne' (1671–1743)

'pericranium': (*Latin*) brain

Book 11 Chapter 9

Sophia and Mrs Fitzpatrick travel to London in the Irish peer's coach.

NOTES AND GLOSSARY:

levee: ceremonial reception at the rising of a great man, for instance a king

artificer: skilled craftsman

drum-room: a room in which a 'drum' or loud late-night party has been held

taper master: a thin or slim youth

'quantum': (*Latin*) allowance, amount

at Eshur, at Stowe . . . : Fielding lists some of the glories of neo-classical architecture and landscape gardening

Boeotian: the Boeotians of ancient Greece were proverbial for their stupidity

Book 11 Chapter 10

Mrs Fitzpatrick looks like becoming the Irish peer's mistress. Sophia moves in with Lady Bellaston.

NOTES AND GLOSSARY:
not better than she should be: a common way of implying sexual promiscuity in women

Book 12 Chapter 1

This chapter is an essay on plagiarism.

NOTES AND GLOSSARY:
Abbé Bannier: a French author (1643–1741) whose *Mythologie* was translated into English in 1739–41
Parnassus: the mountain in Greece sacred to the Muses
Homer, Virgil, Horace, Cicero . . . : see General glossary
Mr Moore: James Moore Smythe (1702–34) borrowed some · lines of Pope for use in his play *The Rival Modes* (1727) for which he was satirised in Pope's great attack on his enemies *The Dunciad* (1728)

Book 12 Chapter 2

Squire Western's pursuit of Sophia is diverted by a hunt. He decides to go home.

NOTES AND GLOSSARY:
'compos voti':   (*Latin*) in possession of what you want
Sir Roger L'Estrange: this is taken from his edition of Aesop, complete with 'reflections', of 1692

Book 12 Chapter 3

Tom and Partridge set out for the wars, the latter reluctantly and the former in gloom.
    Some of the Latin in this chapter has not been translated (according to the usual practice in these Notes), where it is either translated by Fielding or is one of Partridge's commonplace tags. Partridge talks of 'my grammar' in the last paragraph here; he means of course his Latin grammar and is probably referring to *Lily's Grammar*, a standard grammar for schoolboys between the early sixteenth century, when it was written, and the nineteenth century.

NOTES AND GLOSSARY:
'sed vox ea . . .':   (*Latin*) but that is the only word that comes to mind
'mors omnibus communis': (*Latin*) death is common to all
'non immunes . . .': (*Latin*) we are not immune from that ill
'Vir bonus est quis? . . . servat': (*Latin*) who is the good man? He who
follows his fathers and obeys the laws and the rules

Book 12 Chapter 4

Tom and Partridge find Sophia's pocket-book and her one-hundred-pound bill.

NOTES AND GLOSSARY:
toyman: a pedlar selling trinkets, cheap jewels, and other small items
action of trover: legal claim to something that has been found
'orandum est . . . sano': (*Latin*) it is to be prayed for that he is healthy in mind and body

Book 12 Chapter 5

Tom and Partridge come to a town, see a rather dull puppet show and go to an alehouse.

NOTES AND GLOSSARY:
'mens sana . . . sano': (*Latin*) a healthy mind in a healthy body
Master Punch: the main character in the puppet show

Book 12 Chapter 6

The puppet-man's morality. Tom and Partridge stay the night in an alehouse.

NOTES AND GLOSSARY:
Merry-Andrew: clown
Jephtha's Rash Vow: Jephtha vowed to sacrifice whatever he first saw on his return home after a battle, if he won it. He did, and saw his daughter first, being obliged to sacrifice her (see the Bible, Judges, 11 and 12)

Book 12 Chapter 7

The conversation in the alehouse kitchen after Tom has gone to bed displays Jacobite sympathies.

NOTES AND GLOSSARY:

as mad as a March hare: a proverb, which no doubt originates from the springtime courtship antics of the hare

'felix quem . . .': (*Latin*) happy is he who is made cautious by the dangers of others

seized of a right: an obsolete legal phrase, meaning 'possessed of a right'

Papishes . . . Papists . . . Popish: all derogatory ways of referring to Roman Catholicism

Presbyterians: Puritans; 'lower' than Anglicans, that is, Christians more concerned with the Bible than with Bishops

Odsooks!: an imprecation of little specific meaning

Book 12 Chapter 8

Tom and Partridge continue after Sophia. In another alehouse they receive more news of her.

At the end of the paragraph opening 'But so matters fell out . . .' Fielding refers to 'the purpose of this whole work', which is to inculcate a certain 'doctrine'. However, it is not altogether clear from this passage exactly what this doctrine is. It must have some relationship with Fielding's presentation of Tom's 'nature' and seems to suggest a path of common sense between excessive moralising on the one hand and the universal excusing of actions on deterministic grounds on the other.

NOTES AND GLOSSARY:

party-coloured: in motley, wearing brightly coloured and checked clothes

choler: anger

plaister: plaster, covering for a wound

Book 12 Chapter 9

Tom and Partridge follow Sophia's route another stage.

NOTES AND GLOSSARY:

bait: food for horses

Book 12 Chapter 10

Tom meets Lawyer Dowling and tells him of the true position between himself, Allworthy and Blifil.

Notice Jones's comment on Blifil: 'I thought he wanted that generosity of spirit, which is the sure foundation of all that is great and noble in human nature'. Note also the 'compliance' of Tom's 'disposition', that is, he is amenable, readier to say 'yes' than 'no'.

NOTES AND GLOSSARY:

I have a borough for him . . . : in the eighteenth century most Members of Parliament represented 'boroughs' which, in some cases, could be very small indeed. A landlord who owned all the property in a borough could naturally get any candidate of his elected. Dowling has probably bought some freehold property in a small borough and with it has gained control over the votes

Othello . . . Desdemona: in Shakespeare's play Othello is a good deal older than the young Desdemona and wins her love partly by his descriptions of his youthful and manly exploits

Lalage: the woman (Lalagen) referred to in the lines from Horace just quoted. It was a commonplace of classical poetry to attribute a pretty name to the object of a love poem

Book 12 Chapter 11

Tom and Partridge get lost on their way to Coventry.

Notice the list of Fielding's most hated vices at the end of the third paragraph of this chapter. To be a 'fraudulent, griping, cruel, canting miser' is about as low as one can fall, in his estimation. The words imply dishonesty, meanness and hypocrisy as well as something that is quite the opposite of charity.

NOTES AND GLOSSARY:

farrier: vet

spicket: spigot

He and his family are now come to the parish: that is, they are so poor that they have to be relieved by official charity administered by parish officers

Book 12 Chapter 12

Tom and Partridge fall in with a gypsy party in a barn. A political discussion takes place.

Notice the broken English of the gypsies. They had (and in some places still have) their own language (Romany). Fielding's rendering of their dialect is easily enough understood if it is read aloud.

Notice also the purpose of this gypsy episode. Fielding is again worrying at the *nature against art* problem. The gypsies come out rather well from a comparison with the London scenes that are soon to follow.

NOTES AND GLOSSARY:

'Jack with a lanthorn': 'Jack o' lantern', a misleading or elusive light, here, perhaps, a ghost

capable only of affecting the upper gallery: credible only to the poorer parts of the audience (see note on p.42)

Egyptians ... gypsies: these wandering folk, called Romanies by themselves, were believed to have come from Egypt originally

nicety: see General glossary

Aeneas: the hero of Virgil's epic poem, the *Aeneid*

'Dum stupet ... uno': (*Latin*) while, amazed and bewildered, he stares, rooted to the spot

regalia: signs or symbols of kingship

Nerva, Trajan ...: (Footnote) emperors ruling Rome at the height of its power

---

Book 12 Chapter 13

Tom and Partridge discuss Latin and honesty.

NOTES AND GLOSSARY:

Longinus: Name attributed (wrongly) to author of late Greek critical work, *On the Sublime*

'fortuna nunqam ... bona': (*Latin*) fortune is not always good

'non longe ... serviunt': (*Latin*) the grammatical dispute between Tom and Partridge is not important in detail, except in so far as we should realise that Tom is in the right about *'alienum'*. Tom's quotation simply indicates that hanging, mentioned casually by Partridge, is very much to the point. Hanging was a punishment for theft and keeping someone's property from them is theft

'in foro conscientiae': (*Latin*) in the forum of the conscience (in conscience's court)

'fas & nefas': (*Latin*) right and wrong

'Polly matete ...': a Greek tag mispronounced by Partridge. The meaning is that students often know more than their teachers

'nemo omnibus ...': (*Latin*) nobody is right all the time

Book 12 Chapter 14

Tom and Partridge meet a highwayman.

Notice the danger inherent in being a highwayman in the eighteenth century when even ordinary robbery was punishable by death. This man must be desperate indeed.

Notice Fielding's care to establish Tom's strength, courage and generosity at this point just before he plunges into London. It is this fine episode which will lay the foundations of his final winning of Sophia.

NOTES AND GLOSSARY:

St Albans, Barnet: Tom is now in the northern suburbs of modern London although the city in 1750, with a population of 600,000, did not extend quite to Barnet, as the remoteness required for highway robbery makes plain enough

Book 13 Chapter 1

An invocation to some modern muses that Fielding may be helped to write realistically and effectively.

Notice that invocations, set at the head of classical and neo-classical epics (see the opening of Milton's epic poem *Paradise Lost* (1667) for a famous English example) are here parodied at the start of this third and final section of *Tom Jones*. Fielding invokes love of fame and love of money, appropriate to the London section of his work.

NOTES AND GLOSSARY:

Mnesis: Mnemosyne, memory, mother of the muses

Hebrus: a river in Thrace supposed to be a source of inspiration for poets

Maeonia ... Mantua: the supposed birth-place of Homer in Greece and birth-place of Virgil in Italy, respectively

Milton: see General glossary

Charlotte: Fielding's beloved wife

'trachtchugt': (*Dutch*) a canal-boat

'Ufrow Gelt': (*Dutch*) Mrs Money

Grub-street: associated with impoverished authors—much as we now talk of 'Fleet Street' when referring to newspapers in general

Aristophanes ... Marivaux: Fielding lists some great comic and satirical writers. It is perhaps a little odd that he omits Samuel Butler, the author of *Hudibras*, and Ben Jonson from the list

thy Allen and thy Lyttleton: Fielding's friends and patrons (see the first notes on the Dedication)

thy Etonian banks . . .: Eton, the famous public school, is near the Thames at Windsor

thy birchen altar . . .: at the place where he was 'birched' or beaten. Fielding took this punishment in 'Spartan' style, that is, without complaint, like the tough inhabitants of Sparta in Greece

Warburton: Thomas Warburton (1698–1779), editor of Shakespeare and Pope

Book 13 Chapter 2

Tom searches for Sophia in London.

NOTES AND GLOSSARY:

Dr Misaubin: a French doctor of the period before Fielding

direction: address

Sydenham: Mutter suggests Dr Thomas Sydenham (1624–89). A new translation of Sydenham's works had appeared in 1742

Elysian fields: Elysium was the Greek name for paradise; intended ironically

fustian: cheap cloth

Cerberus: in the sixth book of Virgil's *Aeneid* the Sybil leads Aeneas into Hell by drugging the dog-monster, Cerberus ('the keeper of the Stygian avenue')

picquet: a card game, generally for two players only

her sister Abigail: although this could mean 'her sister, whose name was Abigail,' here the meaning is clearly 'her fellow-servant'. 'Abigail' was used to refer to female servants, much as 'Tommy' can refer to soldiers. Read as 'her sister-Abigail'

Book 13 Chapter 3

Mrs Fitzpatrick visits Lady Bellaston and they agree to keep Tom ignorant of the whereabouts of Sophia.

Book 13 Chapter 4

Tom visits Mrs Fitzpatrick, still in vain pursuit of Sophia.

Tom, superior in any rustic situation, is at first made to seem a little awkward in London.

Book 13 Chapter 5

Tom meets Nightingale; their lodgings and Nightingale are described.
Notice the final paragraph of this chapter. Tom is most impressed by Nightingale's 'sentiments of . . . generosity and Humanity' as well as by his susceptibility to love.

NOTES AND GLOSSARY:

scrub: a mean and insignificant person

'vertu': (*French*) prowess, not necessarily in virtuous pursuits

Will's . . . Button's: London coffee-houses of the time

Broughton's amphitheatre: a boxing-school run by Jack Broughton, champion boxer in Fielding's day

you have been upon the stage: you have learnt boxing

muffles: boxing-gloves

his master . . . ordered his man to strip: servants wore 'livery', clothes provided by their masters, sometimes with distinguishing marks on it. Here the 'stripping' would be simply a giving up of the servant's coat to his master, symbolising the end of his employment

four gentlemen of the cloth at whisk: four servants (in the 'cloth' of livery) playing whist

'Hoyle': Edmund Hoyle (1672–1769) published several books on card-games

Arcadian: Arcadian shepherds in classical tradition were forever falling in love with shepherdesses

Book 13 Chapter 6

Tom is invited to a masquerade, but he is penniless.

NOTES AND GLOSSARY:

domino: here, a cloak used for the purpose of disguise

crape: here, the black cloth worn by Anglican clergy

Lombard St: traditionally the centre of banking in the City of London

White's Chocolate House: the equivalent of a modern gentleman's club, similar to a coffee-house

Book 13 Chapter 7

Tom goes to the masquerade. He meets Lady Bellaston and becomes her lover.

'Gallantry to ladies' (everything up to and including fornication) is among Tom's 'principles of honour' and an 'amour' is to be accepted just as a duel would be (see the paragraph opening 'Jones had never . . .'). Now neither of these aspects of 'honour', nor indeed the concept of honour itself, has any place in the Christian moral scheme which is the apparent mainspring of Fielding's message. Perhaps there is a contradiction in it, but Fielding seems to need to add the manly virtues of sexual love and courage to the Christian virtues. Certainly it would be hard, if Tom were a milksop, to admire him as we do.

We can compare *Tom Jones* with *Joseph Andrews* in this light. Joseph is a simpler man than Tom and he manages to preserve his chastity although at the same time it is evident that he is strongly interested in women.

NOTES AND GLOSSARY:

Heydegger ... 'arbiter deliciarum': J.J. Heydegger, a Swiss, was Master of Revels to George II. In this capacity he organised masquerades, balls, operas and other entertainments. As such he is the 'arbiter' of enjoyments or 'judge of pleasures'

spleen: bad temper. All sorts of nervous diseases and depressions were called 'the spleen' in the eighteenth century

the mask walked hastily . . .: here, of course, 'the mask' refers to the person in the mask

Book 13 Chapter 8

Tom and Nightingale hear Mrs Miller's story of her poor cousin Anderson and his family. They have different reactions. Tom is generous: notice that his reaction to distress is at once to give away *all* his money in spite of his own poverty.

NOTES AND GLOSSARY:

a competency: an income
cawdle: comforting, warm and medicinal drink
sold by an execution: sold by an order of court
50l: fifty pounds
pitiful largesses: inadequate charitable donations

Book 13 Chapter 9

Tom is seen in the role of Lady Bellaston's lover.

NOTES AND GLOSSARY:
Papists: Catholics
French novels: these were supposed to be specially immoral
she had, besides, a certain imperfection . . .: the implication here is that Lady Bellaston does not smell very nice. People did not wash very much in the eighteenth century, and Dr Johnson was probably speaking no more than the truth when he said, in reply to a lady who told him that he smelled, 'No madam, you smell; I stink'
Methodist: see note to Book 1 Chapter 10

Book 13 Chapter 10

Tom visits Anderson, who turns out to be the 'highwayman' who accosted him near Barnet.

Fielding demonstrates how virtue leads to happiness: Tom's generosity has led to 'a sweeter pleasure, than the ambitious, the avaricious, or the voluptuous man can ever obtain': all this and heaven too.

Book 13 Chapter 11

Tom at last meets Sophia, by accident, at Lady Bellaston's.

NOTES AND GLOSSARY:
a young booby squire: a young and stupid country gentleman

Book 13 Chapter 12

Lady Bellaston and Sophia discuss Tom, neither admitting that she knows him, though one is his lover and the other his love.

NOTES AND GLOSSARY:
Lord Shaftesbury: author of *Characteristics*, in which humanity and charity are put before honesty in some cases

Book 14 Chapter 1

Fielding tells us that authors should know something about the subjects they treat. In this case we are dealing with high society.

NOTES AND GLOSSARY:
Homer or Virgil: see General glossary
Pitt: William Pitt the elder (1708–78), Prime Minister later in his life. He was a friend of Fielding

Demosthenes and Cicero: respectively, Greek and Roman orators

Bysse's 'Art of Poetry': Edward Bysse's critical anthology of 1702

'quam quisque . . .': (*Latin*) people should do what they know best how to do

Thucydides . . . Livy: respectively, great Greek and Roman historians. Thucydides (*c.*460–*c.*400BC) chronicled the Peloponnesian War between Athens and Sparta; Livy (59BC–AD17) wrote a History of Rome from its foundation to 9BC

Mr Essex . . . : a book by Essex appeared in 1722 entitled *The Young Ladies' Conduct, or Rules for Education*

Mr Broughton: see note to Book 13 Chapter 5

Vanbrugh and Congreve: Restoration dramatists (see Part 1, Introduction, pp.6–7)

Hogarth . . . Titian . . . Vandyke: painters specialising in human subjects. For William Hogarth (1697–1764) see General glossary. Tiziano Vecelli (*c.*1490–1576) was the greatest of the Venetian painters. Sir Anthony Van Dyck (1599–1641) was from Flanders; a great portrait painter, he became Court Painter to Charles I of England

the centaur, the chimera: mythological creatures

what Mr Pope says of women: in his *Moral Essays* Pope claims that 'most women have no characters at all'

Beau Monde: the upper classes

Book 14 Chapter 2

Lady Bellaston visits Tom; more intrigues.
 Notice that this chapter is like a scene from a play.

NOTES AND GLOSSARY:

The reversion: the basic right; the other woman will get Tom in the end

---

Book 14 Chapter 3

Tom finds himself in a dilemma between his two women.
 Fielding shows his mastery of rapid dialogue in this chapter; this is perhaps another legacy of his days as a playwright.

Book 14 Chapter 4

Tom has to leave Mrs Miller's because of Lady Bellaston's visit.

NOTES AND GLOSSARY:
to bilk my lodgings: to leave without paying
the two pair of stairs: that is, two floors up; the second floor
a certain mystery, called 'Making Love': this phrase referred only to flirtation and to conversational approaches between two people in the eighteenth and nineteenth centuries

Book 14 Chapter 5

Mrs Miller's story is told.

The insertion of this tale reinforces the novel's conception of goodness; here it is of Mr Allworthy's goodness that we learn.

Book 14 Chapter 6

Tom and the whole household discover that Nancy is pregnant by the now departed Nightingale.

Notice the paradox that to be compassionate one must in some way be *weak* (see the first paragraph of this chapter—'poor Jones ... had all that weakness which is called compassion ...'

NOTES AND GLOSSARY:
bowl: wooden ball, as in the game of bowls
Foundling Hospital: an institution established for the care of abandoned children and bastards

Book 14 Chapter 7

Tom and Nightingale have an impassioned discussion of what is right conduct.

Notice the significance of the discussion between these two young men. Tom displays a talent for seeing things straight: honour, honesty and humanity all point to one and the same course of action and he says so. Nightingale is a normal sort of man, not bad but not very good. Tom, by contrast, is morally keen-sighted and quite exceptionally good, especially as his own behaviour, without ever being pious, has been based on the morality he here preaches.

Book 14 Chapter 8

Tom and old Mr Nightingale's brother try to convince old Mr Nightingale to act generously towards Nancy and his son by pretending that they are already married.

NOTES AND GLOSSARY:
the Roman satyrist: Juvenal (see General glossary)
Seneca: see General glossary
Cicero: see General glossary
to over-reach: to outdo in bargaining
St Antony: of Padua; he preached to the fishes
Orpheus and Amphion: according to classical mythology both had miraculous gifts of music

Book 14 Chapter 9

Old Mr Nightingale's brother, on discovering that Nancy and Nightingale are not in fact married, tries to dissuade Nightingale from marrying her.

Notice the seemingly exaggerated importance given to old Mr Nightingale's brother. The point seems to be that, rather as in the old comedy of humours, Fielding needs a new character to represent a new point of view, and here he wants someone to display a half-way stage between the intransigence of old Mr Nightingale and the decency of Nightingale himself once Tom has put his duty before him.

Book 14 Chapter 10

Tom is suspicious as Nightingale goes off with his uncle.

Book 15 Chapter 1

Fielding observes that virtue does not necessarily lead to happiness in this world.

NOTES AND GLOSSARY:
Epicureans . . . epicures: the exalted philosophy of Epicurus (341–270BC), founder of a Greek school of thought, for whom virtue led to the highest good (peace of mind). His philosophy was pursued as such by his followers (Epicureans), but became debased in popular thought to include those who believed that the best thing for man was to eat, drink and be merry (epicures)

Book 15 Chapter 2

Lord Fellamar falls in love with Sophia and schemes with Lady Bellaston to get her.

NOTES AND GLOSSARY:

you have struck a damp into my heart: you have planted a disese in my heart

past three in the morning: Fielding seems to mean here that, although the time is clearly three pm, it is rendered 'morning' by the (new?) habit of dining after midday. Dinner traditionally separated morning from afternoon, a distinction that became less and less tenable as dinner got later and later

Book 15 Chapter 3

Lord Fellamar and Lady Bellaston pursue their scheme.

NOTES AND GLOSSARY:

the late war: the War of the Austrian Succession, which finished in 1748

a rubbers at whist: that is, a game of cards

Shakespeare: the lines are from *Julius Caesar*

Book 15 Chapter 4

Lord Fellamar's doubts about Sophia are removed. He resolves to conquer her by force.

NOTES AND GLOSSARY:

Newgate solicitors: Newgate was the main prison of central London. The implication here is that lawyers too closely associated with its criminal fraternity might suborn witnesses on behalf of their clients

Helen . . . Paris: the cause of the Trojan war was, of course, the abduction (or 'rape') of Helen by Paris

the Sabine ladies: they were abducted, according to legend, by the Romans, who were short of wives

Mr Hook: a historian of Rome. His *Roman History* was published in 1738

Book 15 Chapter 5

Sophia is saved from Lord Fellamar's attempt at rape only by the arrival of her father, who carries her off.

Notice Western's dialect. 'Shat ha un' = 'Thou shalt have him', 'You will (must) have him'. 'Spit' refers to Lord Fellamar's sword. 'My grannum' is 'my grandmother'.

NOTES AND GLOSSARY:

'The Fatal Marriage': a play by Thomas Southerne (1659-1746), performed 1694

bombast: excessive speech

myrmidons: troops, assistants in battle

crown: here, five shillings; twenty-five new pence

Book 15 Chapter 6

This chapter describes how Squire Western came to find his daughter.

NOTES AND GLOSSARY:

in Holland, when Lewis the Fourteenth . . . : Louis XIV of France (reigned 1643-1715) besieged Amsterdam in 1672

Quotha!: she says!

Size: here, the assizes, the law court in the country

Hannover law: the law of the Georges and the 'Hanover rats' rather than the law of the 'true' Jacobite kings

'je vous mesprise . . .': (*French*) I despise you with all my heart

Greenland . . . Tramontane: Greenland, which had only recently been colonised by Denmark, was of course quite the reverse of 'polite'. 'Tramontane' means 'barbarian'

Book 15 Chapter 7

Tom is surprised by Lady Bellaston who catches him talking to Mrs Honour. Lady Bellaston starts to give him up.

Book 15 Chapter 8

Tom sees Nancy and Nightingale married.

NOTES AND GLOSSARY:

Doctors Commons: an ecclesiastical court in London where marriage licences were issued. In *David Copperfield* (1850) Charles Dickens (1812-70) calls it a 'rotten old ecclesiastical cheese'

Terence: Roman comic playwright (190-159BC)

'homo sum . . . puto': (*Latin*) I am a man: I do not consider anything human to be alien from me

Book 15 Chapter 9

Tom finds a way out of his entanglement with Lady Bellaston.

NOTES AND GLOSSARY:
demirep: a woman of questionable reputation or chastity
tittle-tattle: gossip

Book 15 Chapter 10

Mr Allworthy warns that he is coming to London; Mrs Honour enters Lady Bellaston's service.

Notice the execrable English of Mrs Honour's letter. If in doubt, read it aloud and the meaning will become clear.

NOTES AND GLOSSARY:
Prior: Matthew Prior (1664–1721), poet, essayist and diplomat
Old Bailey: the main criminal court in London
Addison: Joseph Addison (1672–1719), essayist and poet. The line is from his tragedy *Cato* (1713)
'verbatim & literatim': (*Latin*) word for word and letter for letter

---

Book 15 Chapter 11

Tom is proposed to by Arabella Hunt, but 'nature' prevails and he rejects her offer.

This episode seems to be inserted to demonstrate Tom's fortitude and his worthiness of Sophia's hand.

NOTES AND GLOSSARY:
she owned six and twenty: she admitted herself to be twenty-six years old (although she was in fact thirty)
an old Turkey merchant: a trader with the Middle East; not a poulterer
billet: here, note
I doubt my eyes have told you . . . : 'doubt' here means 'fear'
dunned: pressed repeatedly for money

Book 15 Chapter 12

Partridge discovers that Sophia is still in London. Tom writes her a letter which is conveyed by Black George.

NOTES AND GLOSSARY:
'Non sum qualis eram': (*Latin*) I am not as I used to be
'ad unguem': (*Latin*) on the nail: an example of Partridge's cockeyed use of Latin

Book 16 Chapter 1

This is an essay on prologues to plays and novels.

Book 16 Chapter 2

Squire Western refuses a challenge from Lord Fellamar and argues further with Sophia about her marriage.

Notice the system of duelling common in the eighteenth century. If a gentleman felt that his honour had been insulted he would send a 'second' (here the captain) to challenge the offender. If the offender did not apologise he would have to meet his challenger and duel with him. The captain here starts by asking for a 'trifling acknowledgement' by Western that his insult to Lord Fellamar was due to alcohol; when the squire will not give this he tries to insist on a duel and when this is refused Western is supposedly branded a coward.

Notice Western's dialect again ('varden' = 'farthing'—that is, $\frac{1}{4}$d, a quarter of an old penny).

NOTES AND GLOSSARY:

the turnkey of Newgate: the prison officer at the main prison in London

Book 16 Chapter 3

Sophia receives Tom's letter from Black George.

NOTES AND GLOSSARY:

The Royal Society: a scientific body, founded in 1660, often ridiculed by Fielding

Ovid . . . Virgil: in the *Metamorphoses* Ovid tells of Hyacinthus's blood being changed into a flower when he was killed. There were letters on the leaves reading 'Ai' —'woe!' Virgil mentions this story in his *Eclogues*

maw: mouth

'academies des sciences': the European equivalents of the Royal Society

Book 16 Chapter 4

Mrs Western arrives in London, quarrels with her brother, sets Sophia free and takes her to her own lodgings.

Mrs Western uses military and political metaphor throughout this episode, for instance 'evacuate the garrison' for 'go away'.

NOTES AND GLOSSARY:

Turnpike acts: turnpikes were toll-gates on main roads, looked after by committees created by Act of Parliament. The roads were supposed to be better than other roads which were looked after by the local parishes individually

Thalestris . . . Amazons: see note to Book 9 Chapter 3

Babble . . . whip thee in . . . : hunting terms: dogs 'babble' (bark) and have to be controlled ('whipped in')

julap: a sweet drink, especially one used to cool the passions

choler: anger

capuchin: a hooded cloak

Book 16 Chapter 5

Tom receives a letter from Sophia; he takes Partridge to see *Hamlet*; Partridge's reactions.

NOTES AND GLOSSARY:

consumption: the disease tuberculosis, a common killer in the eighteenth and nineteenth centuries

Platonic affection: non-sexual love

Common-Prayer Book: the Anglican book of Church services, including a service of thanksgiving introduced after the failure of the Gunpowder Plot of 1605

Garrick: see note to Book 7 Chapter 1

'Nulla fides fronti': (*Latin*) do not trust the appearances of things

Book 16 Chapter 6

This chapter is a retrospect, showing how Allworthy and Blifil have come to London to try again with Sophia.

Notice the penultimate paragraph of this chapter ('Thus did the affection . . .') in which Fielding makes the admission that Mr Allworthy is lacking in perception.

Book 16 Chapter 7

Western and Blifil call on Sophia, with little result.

NOTES AND GLOSSARY:

Odsbud!: a politer way of saying 'God's body!', an imprecation

Book 16 Chapter 8

Lord Fellamar and Lady Bellaston plot for the undoing of Tom. Lady Bellaston visits Mrs Western and they plot the eradication of Tom from Sophia's affections.

NOTES AND GLOSSARY:

Some method of having him pressed: a way to have him taken up by the press-gang, the official group who went about finding suitable men and forcing them to join the navy

'carte blanche': (*French*) freedom to do as one wishes. Here Fellamar is offering the Western family any conditions they choose in regard to the financial arrangements of his marriage to Sophia

Hottentot: that is, savage, barbarian

Book 16 Chapter 9

Mrs Fitzpatrick suggests to Tom that he should court Mrs Western as a route to obtaining her niece. Tom rejects the suggestion, and also refuses to take up the hints of love Mrs Fitzpatrick makes.

Notice that Tom is again tempted and again resists.

NOTES AND GLOSSARY:

liquorish: lively; here, sexually

Oroondates: a vociferous character in La Calprenède's ten-volume romance *Cassandra* (1647-56)

Book 16 Chapter 10

Tom duels with Mr Fitzpatrick and seems to kill him, for which he is arrested. In prison he learns that Sophia has seen his letter proposing marriage to Lady Bellaston.

This chapter marks the lowest ebb in the changing tide of Tom's fortunes.

NOTES AND GLOSSARY:

that green-eyed monster ... 'Othello': jealousy, the affliction from which Othello suffers and which is his undoing

a number of fellows rushed in and seized Jones: this is the press-gang threatened two chapters earlier; hence their remarks such as 'he's bound to another port now'

the Gate-house: a prison in Westminster

Book 17 Chapter 1

'To natural means alone we are confined' in our attempt to get a happy ending, says Fielding.

NOTES AND GLOSSARY:
'felo de se':   (*Latin*) his own enemy (used of suicides)
Tyburn: see note to Book 8 Chapter 1

Book 17 Chapter 2

Mrs Miller starts to open Mr Allworthy's eyes to the true nature of Tom, but she is interrupted.

NOTES AND GLOSSARY:
Plutarch: a Greek historian who lived during the first century AD. His biographies of Greek and Roman worthies (*Lives*) were the source for several plays by Shakespeare and others

Book 17 Chapter 3

Squire Western and Mr Allworthy discuss what to do with Sophia. Blifil's machinations start to catch up with him.

NOTES AND GLOSSARY:
Od-rat-it: for 'God rot it'
One Acton . . . :   the ignorant Western mistakes this name. He means Actaeon who, in Greek legend, was destroyed by his own hounds after Diana had turned him into a stag as a punishment for having seen her bathing
Doctors Commons: see note to Book 15 Chapter 8

Book 17 Chapter 4

Sophia and Mrs Western discuss Lord Fellamar.

NOTES AND GLOSSARY:
Parthenissa: poets from the Renaissance to the nineteenth century have given their mistresses fanciful classical names. Here Mrs Western goes the length of saying that this name of hers was frequently engraved on windows—a custom not unknown but surely not as common as her memory tells her

Tully Cicero: Marcus Tullius Cicero (see General glossary) is generally called Cicero or 'Tully', not both

Book 17 Chapter 5

Mrs Miller and Partridge visit Tom in prison.

Book 17 Chapter 6

Mrs Miller visits Sophia with Tom's letter. Sophia has to spend an evening with Lady Bellaston and Lord Fellamar.

NOTES AND GLOSSARY:
Lady Thomas Hatchet's drum: the reader is recommended to consult Fielding's own definition of this type of party in the last four paragraphs of the chapter

Book 17 Chapter 7

Mrs Miller again begins to justify Tom to Mr Allworthy.

NOTES AND GLOSSARY:
pathetic: affecting

Book 17 Chapter 8

Lord Fellamar tries again with Sophia, to no avail. Mrs Western resolves to return Sophia to her father.

NOTES AND GLOSSARY:
like the wise King of Prussia: Frederick the Great (1712–86) repudiated his allies in the War of the Austrian Succession and declared himself to be neutral

Book 17 Chapter 9

Mrs Waters visits Tom in prison. She tells him that Fitzpatrick, with whom she is now living, is out of danger.

NOTES AND GLOSSARY:
hedge-tavern: poor inn frequented by disreputable people
The Devil when he was sick: presumably a reference to the sentiment, found in Rabelais and elsewhere, that the devil will be good and repentant when sick but not otherwise

Book 18 Chapter 1

Fielding's farewell to the reader. There is a touch of self-justification here. Fielding offers to lay aside his jesting and digressions in favour of simple narrative. This is needed to bring all the threads of the tale together, but it also gives this last book the rather starker character of a Book of Judgement in which all are suitably rewarded.

Book 18 Chapter 2

Partridge tells Tom that Mrs Waters is Tom's mother. Can he have committed incest? Sophia is now back at Squire Western's.

NOTES AND GLOSSARY:

If the reader will please to refresh his memory . . .: Fielding does not simply say that Partridge never met Mrs Waters at Upton; he chooses, instead, to draw our attention to the 'ninth book' of his novel. This is typical of his selfconscious style of narration

Billingsgate: the London fish-market, famous for the bad language of its employees

Book 18 Chapter 3

Mr Allworthy reconciles old Mr Nightingale to seeing his son and discovers the five hundred pounds stolen by Black George from Tom early in the novel. Allworthy begins seriously to relent towards Tom.

NOTES AND GLOSSARY:

the Black Act: part of the Game Laws prescribing death for certain violations of them

Book 18 Chapter 4

Letters from Square and Thwackum to Mr Allworthy tending to exonerate Tom.

NOTES AND GLOSSARY:

Dr Harrington . . . Dr Brewster: these were actual doctors at Bath

Plato . . . Cicero: see General glossary

the living of Westerton: the job of vicar or priest, being attached to a specific parish, came to be known as the 'living' of that parish. Thwackum already has one living and clearly wants another: this sort of plurality was a

notorious abuse in the Church of England in the
eighteenth century. Livings were often, as here, in
the gift of landowners

Book 18 Chapter 5

Blifil, suspected of treachery, scrapes together an excuse. Mr Allworthy
has a conversation with Partridge.

NOTES AND GLOSSARY:
pressed on board a ship: conscripted involuntarily into the navy
Old Bailey: the main criminal court in London
'Non sum qualis eram': (*Latin*) I am not as I was. The point is that Allworthy does indeed know that Partridge was a
schoolmaster

Book 18 Chapter 6

Partridge tells Allworthy the full story of his misfortunes and those
of Tom.

NOTES AND GLOSSARY:
Size: the assizes, courts periodically set up in the country

Book 18 Chapter 7

Mrs Waters tells Mr Allworthy the full story of Tom's birth and reveals,
by chance, Blifil's villainy.
    In these two chapters (6 and 7) Mr Allworthy is put in the position of
a judge. Gradually all the evidence is being assembled before him.

Book 18 Chapter 8

Mrs Waters and Mr Allworthy continue. Squire Western interrupts
and Allworthy offers to talk to Sophia. Dowling appears and Allworthy
gets the truth out of him.

NOTES AND GLOSSARY:
Doctor Faustus: Squire Western is merely using this name as part of
an oath. In the German legend Faustus sold his
soul to the devil
His goodness . . .: in the third paragraph of this chapter, Fielding says
that Mr Allworthy's goodness is more like that of
God than that of man

Book 18 Chapter 9

Mr Allworthy offers Tom to Sophia who, to his surprise, rejects him. Squire Western, now abreast of events, takes Tom's side.

Notice how important it is for Sophia at this point to reject Tom. This is not primarily a love-story but a moral tale; Sophia must be true to herself and not simply fall into the arms of a man she loves if he is unworthy of her.

Book 18 Chapter 10

Mr Allworthy and Tom are reconciled. Mrs Miller holds out some hope that Sophia will relent.

In the last paragraph of this chapter Fielding admits to being in a greater hurry now that he is moving towards his conclusion.

NOTES AND GLOSSARY:

Seneca:	see General glossary
A't:	this from Squire Western means 'art', as in 'thou art' ('you are')

Book 18 Chapter 11

Blifil is banished. Mr Allworthy stands for justice and Tom pleads for mercy. Compare the end of Shakespeare's *Measure for Measure*.

Notice the debate between justice and mercy here. The impression given is that Mr Allworthy is a stern God-the-Father figure while Tom intercedes like God-the-Son. For Mr Allworthy 'compassion and forgiveness' can 'become faults' but in pure Christianity this is not so.

NOTES AND GLOSSARY:

Harlequin:	a comic stage character deriving from the Italian *Commedia del'Arte*, a popular improvised style of theatre common in Italy from the sixteenth to the eighteenth centuries

Book 18 Chapter 12

Tom woos Sophia's forgiveness for his infidelities. She says that time must show him faithful and stipulates a year's trial. This period is reduced until, at Squire Western's behest, it becomes a single day. Thus they are to be married tomorrow.

Notice that Tom admits that 'Justice' must condemn him, yet Sophia does not do so in the end.

Notice that Tom, having been expelled from Paradise Hall early in the novel, finds his 'heaven' at the end of it in Sophia's 'dear bosom'. Notice that even Fielding seems to think that the romantic strain has been pitched rather high in the conversation between Tom and Sophia and seems to enjoy the relief of coming down to earth when Squire Western bursts in to put an end to Sophia's 'flim flam' (nonsense).

NOTES AND GLOSSARY:
ha' the tousling her: be her first lover
a Dorimant, a Lord Rochester: Dorimant is a character in Etherege's comedy *The Man of Mode* (1676). He is partly modelled on Lord Rochester, a rake and poet of the Restoration period
shill I shall I, dilly dally: that is, indecisively

Chapter the last

Happy, or rather, suitable endings are granted to all.

NOTES AND GLOSSARY:
Doctors Commons: see note to Book 15 Chapter 8
Mr Abraham Adams: the parson who is perhaps the principal character in Fielding's earlier novel, *Joseph Andrews* (1742). Adams, based on a friend of Fielding's, is perfectly simple-hearted and delightfully benevolent

General glossary

admire: be surprised at
amour: love-affair
Aristotle: Greek philosopher (384–322BC) whose lectures on tragedy, now known as the *Poetics*, contain suggested rules for literary composition many of which are broken by Fielding, as he acknowledges
Bridewell: a London prison of the period, particularly for women; also used generally to mean 'prison'
buss: kiss
Butler: Samuel Butler (1612–80), one of Fielding's favourite modern authors. His *Hudibras* (1663–78) is a satirical poem in which, as in *Tom Jones*, hypocrisy and selfishness are ridiculed and puritanism criticised. *Hudibras* owes much to *Don Quixote* and is a mock-heroic poem rather as that novel is mock-chivalric

Cervantes:	Miguel de Cervantes (1547–1616), author of *Don Quixote* and a model for Fielding
character:	can mean 'reputation'
Cicero:	Marcus Tullius Cicero (106–43BC), Roman orator, letter-writer and essayist
complaisant (complacent):	wanting to please
complexion:	nature, especially of humans; thus a 'warm complexion' is a volatile, amorous and perhaps argumentative nature
condescension:	politeness to inferiors (not pejorative)
coxcomb:	foolish and impertinent fellow
decent:	modest; seemly
Demosthenes:	Greek orator (383–322BC)
discover:	to reveal to others
doth:	does
exquisite:	extreme (especially of pain), exact, refined
family:	the whole household, especially the servants
friends:	one's family, not one's friends
grateful:	pleasing
guinea:	one pound and one shilling, twenty-one shillings (£1.05p)
hartshorn:	an ammonia-based restorative, like smelling-salts
hath:	has
Hogarth:	William Hogarth (1697–1764), painter and engraver. He engraved the illustrations for an edition of *Hudibras* (1726) and then several great series of prints, for instance, 'The Harlot's Progress', 'The Rake's Progress' and 'Marriage à la Mode'. These showed a fiercely satirical and moral element that connects him easily with his friend Fielding
Homer:	(sixth century BC?) the father of Western literature, probable author of the two great epics the *Iliad*, an account of the Trojan War, and the *Odyssey*, an account of the wanderings of Ulysses after the fall of Troy. These poems contain a great number of stories many of which reappear constantly in Western literature, for instance in Chaucer and Shakespeare. His importance to Fielding is that Fielding, too, is writing an epic, but his is a modern prose comedy of everyday life rather than a grand poem of gods and heroes
honour:	a difficult concept. A man's honour was his reputation for courage, and it required that he would not accept an insult tamely. A woman's honour was

her reputation for virtue. There is, however, an ambiguity in this: if honour is *merely* reputation then it concerns only outward appearance, but the word is frequently used in a far less superficial sense than this would imply and Tom, for instance, is truly a man of honour in that he is not only *apparently* trustworthy but *actually* so. Shakespeare plays with the concept instructively in *2 Henry IV* and *As You Like It*, among other places. See Tom and Nightingale on honour, in Book 14 Chapter 7

Horace: Quintus Horatius Flaccus (65–8BC), Roman poet. His *Ars Poetica* lays down rules further to those of Aristotle. Much debated in the seventeenth and eighteenth centuries, these rules are broken by Fielding, but in a spirit of friendly acknowledgement

'Hudibras':   see 'Butler', above

impertinent: irrelevant

Jove: the senior god in Greek mythology (Jupiter). Used in neo-classical literature as an approximation to 'God'

Juvenal: Decimus Junius Juvenalis (AD60–130), who wrote sixteen satires, extremely sharp denunciations of the Roman society in which he lived. They served as models for the satirists of the seventeenth and eighteenth centuries

liquorish: frisky, especially sexually

Milton: John Milton (1608–74) was important to Fielding (a) because of his high reputation as a puritan poet and (b) because of his attempt, so different from Fielding's own, to write a modern epic. His *Paradise Lost* was composed in the 1660s when he was already blind. His Adam has some points of comparison with Fielding's Tom

Nemesis: the Greek goddess of revenge

nervous: strong

nice: exact, fastidious

nostrum: medicine, generally that prescribed by a fraudulent doctor, or quack

'Odyssey':   Homer's epic of Ulysses's ten-year voyage home to Ithaca after the Trojan war. Ulysses is a type of cunning and endurance, his wife Penelope of patience and fidelity

ostler: groom; one who looks after horses at an inn

Ovid: Publius Ovidius Naso (43BC–AD18), Roman poet particularly associated with love poetry and amorous tales, as, for instance, in his collection, the *Metamorphoses*

pathetic: full of feeling

person: physical person, body, looks

place: job, especially in the case of servants

Plato: Greek philosopher (427–348BC). He was probably important to Fielding as offering a more spiritual and idealist view of the world than Aristotle with his logic. 'Platonic love' is non-sexual

Pope: Alexander Pope (1688–1744), a great poet and satirist contemporary with Fielding, who was also a popular translator of Homer. Pope translated both the *Iliad* and the *Odyssey* with great success and opened these poems up to English readers without Greek

presently: now

proper: suitable, appropriate

receipt: recipe

Seneca: Lucius Annaeus Seneca (*d.* 65AD), Stoic philosopher and tragedian

sensible: able to be felt, sensitive

Socrates: great Greek philosopher (469–399BC). The main character in most of Plato's dialogues; his teachings seem to be those found in Plato's early works. Above all he was concerned with moral questions— how man should live

stagger: to trip someone up; especially metaphorically, as in to be 'staggered in one's opinions'

Swift: Dean Jonathan Swift (1667–1745), satirist, author of *Gulliver's Travels*, *A Tale of a Tub*, *The Battle of the Books* and many pamphlets and poems. In the same mould as Fielding, Swift became a great deal more bitter than his contemporary

Virgil: Publius Vergilius Maro (70–19BC), author of the Roman national epic poem the *Aeneid*, written in imitation of Homer

Part 3

Commentary

Fielding's purpose

Tom Jones has been praised for its structure (by Coleridge) and for its comic qualities; it has also been seen as a true picture of eighteenth-century life and manners. The structure and the comedy, however, are the *means* that Fielding employs, and the picture of contemporary life is a by-product of his method. What, then, is the main *purpose* of the novel? What does Fielding employ these means for? The answer is a simple one: *Tom Jones* is first and foremost a moral novel and Fielding's purpose is to display and to advocate a certain, largely Christian, morality.

As some of the notes in Part 2 of this study will have made clear, every single episode in the novel is treated from a moral point of view; indeed, many of the episodes are introduced exclusively in order to explore or explain a particular moral point. Fielding's own titles for some of his chapters provide us with our first examples. Often enough his titles say little or nothing (for example, 'Being the shortest chapter in this book') but at other times we read whole sentences, such as:

> The Trial of Partridge, the Schoolmaster, for Incontinency; the evidence of his Wife: a short Reflection on the Wisdom of our Law; with other grave Matters, which those will like best who understand them most

or:

> A short Sketch of that Felicity which prudent Couples may extract from Hatred; with a short Apology for those People who overlook Imperfections in their Friends

Our attention is being drawn to areas of moral concern: incontinency, wisdom of the law, hatred and so on. Notice that Fielding does not write, in the second example, 'Captain and Mrs Blifil enjoy hating each other'. Instead he generalises the point to include all 'couples' or, to put it another way, he moralises on it.

Besides these examples there are dozens of others. Thwackum and Square could be just a couple of obsessive characters, but it is quite clear that they are exact moral types, with Thwackum representing a vicious and gluttonous selfishness in spite of his professed Christianity, and Square a very ordinary set of human appetites rendered hypocritical by his self-important stoicism. Blifil and Tom could be a couple of rival lads, one rather nicer than the other, but Fielding goes to great lengths to exhibit them side by side in order to reveal their moral qualities: Tom hurts himself rescuing a bird that Blifil has maliciously released; Tom sells a horse and a Bible to help the poor, Blifil reads the Bible ostentatiously so that, as a result, Tom will get into trouble for it, and so on.

As examples of elements introduced exclusively to make moral points we can consider Anderson (the would-be highwayman of Book 12 who is in fact merely in great distress and who is helped by his intended victim, Tom) and Nightingale, whose behaviour to Nancy, whether taken on its own or as a contrast to Tom's behaviour to Sophia, is clearly intended to make a moral point. It is worth asking whether Anderson and Nightingale can really serve any other purpose than the advancement of Fielding's moral ideas. They do not do much to help the plot and they only confirm the view of Tom that we already hold. Here perhaps is a proof of Fielding's moral purpose.

Fielding's morality: 'good nature'

All this talk of a moral purpose in Fielding must not be allowed to give the impression that he is a pompous, solemn or dogmatic preacher. On the contrary, with the greatest of good humour (and common sense) he shows us how a good-natured scheme of generous and open behaviour is better for everyone, including the person in question, than any form of self-seeking pettiness, meanness, hypocrisy, duplicity or greed.

As each character is introduced he is weighed morally and often shown in action so that we can see whether he lives up to his own professed standards. See, for instance, Book 3 Chapter 3, and Book 5 Chapter 2, where Thwackum and Square are described and put through their paces. The aim here seems to be to build up a general picture of what Fielding calls 'good nature' and of its reverse.

Tom is the model of 'good nature'. He is 'an inoffensive lad amidst all his roguery' but he is 'somewhat passionate in his disposition'. Thus he is not aggressive, but where there is a real challenge to him as a man (either from another man who insults him or attacks someone weaker, or from a woman who challenges him to love) he will take up the challenge without any cowardly or mealy-mouthed hesitation. Then he is spotted by Partridge as being 'one of the best-natured gentlemen in the universe' and in this is included an engaging 'want of caution' and a slight recklessness that stand up well beside Blifil's calculating spirit.

This 'good nature' is largely Christian charity, the cornerstone of

Fielding's morality, but it is a few other things besides, and it is these things which make it quite the opposite of puritan meanness of spirit. To put the point in Mr Allworthy's words we can consult Book 5 Chapter 8, where he says this to Tom: 'I am convinced, my child, that you have much goodness, generosity and honour in your temper; if you will add prudence and religion to these, you must be happy: for the three former qualities, I admit, make you worthy of happiness, but they are the latter only which will put you in possession of it.' These words, from Allworthy on his supposed death-bed, are worth pondering. To the specifically Christian 'goodness' he adds 'generosity' (also Christian, although Tom takes this to a length recommended by few Christians and practised by fewer) and 'honour' (a manly virtue not really Christian at all; see General glossary). He then adds 'prudence', which may not seem very attractive in a novel where *im*prudent behaviour saves Sophia from Blifil, and Tom's own impetuosity is a major source of pleasure; but in truth Tom needs a little of this at least to survive. Next comes 'religion', which must mean something like 'the deliberate practice of religious duties' in addition to those of charity. This last may have been truly a conviction of Fielding's but it must be said that in a novel where all the divines are portrayed in a poor light and where churchgoing is reduced to a social occasion the presence of 'religion' in this sense is not very strong.

Allworthy's list seems to establish Fielding's moral priorities. What is said about 'prudence' and 'religion' is that they enable the man who is *already* virtuous to become happy. From a moral point of view, then, 'goodness, generosity and honour' have an absolute priority, and it is these qualities that constitute 'good nature'. This good nature is a grouping of virtues that tend to hang together. Thus, for instance, Book 11 Chapter 10 contains some very instructive passages on 'suspicion' (that is, thinking badly of people) in connection with Sophia. This aspect of her character might seem marginal to her main virtues, but Fielding is trying to establish her good nature and clearly thinks that this matter of 'suspicion' is as significant a test of character as any other: people with really good natures show themselves to be good under any aspect.

Following from this, one strongly stressed element in Fielding's morality is the necessary connection between appearance and reality. Hypocrisy is one of his most detested vices and it lends an extra dimension of evil to other actions; thus Blifil's malicious attitude to Tom is bad enough but it is rendered intolerable (and temporarily very effective) by his concealment of it behind a mask of virtue. In this context Fielding takes sides very vigorously in the post-reformation argument between 'faith' and 'works'. Roughly speaking, the more extreme the Protestant, the more likely he was to adopt Luther's opinion that faith was enough for salvation even in the absence of good works. This doctrine, which Fielding found understandably detestable, is espoused by Captain Blifil in his dispute with Mr Allworthy in Book 2 Chapter 5, where he undertakes to show that charity should not consist in *actions*. It appears further in Square's character which, in practice, reveals that he went 'so far, as to regard all virtue as matter of theory only' (Book 3 Chapter 4). Captain Blifil and Square are shown to be unvirtuous in the ensuing action. For Fielding faith may have an honourable place, but 'works' (real actions of charity) are infinitely more important.

Finally, these questions of Fielding's moral purpose and his exaltation of good nature over all meanness and hypocrisy are well enough presented by the author himself in his 'Apology', which constitutes Book 3 Chapter 4. After reading that chapter (or indeed almost any other in the novel) it becomes impossible to agree with Dr Johnson's extraordinary condemnation of *Tom Jones* as a 'vicious' book. In no other work of literature, surely, is virtue presented in a more attractive light.

In all this Fielding is indebted to that most humane of moral philosophers, Shaftesbury, whose *Characteristics of Men, Manners, Opinions, Times* of 1711 (revised 1713) contained his famous essay '*An Enquiry concerning Virtue*' of 1699. In this he propounds his ideas of 'moral sense', the quality whereby a man can judge between right and wrong, of the possibility of unselfish action, and of the possibility that the private and public good can coincide.

Eighteenth-century politics

In 1642 civil war broke out in Britain between the followers of King Charles I, the last British king to claim absolute power for the monarch, and the parliamentarians, led by Oliver Cromwell, whose ambition it was to limit royal power. Charles lost the war, was executed in 1649, and left Oliver Cromwell Protector of the Commonwealth of Britain. Shortly after Cromwell's death parliament invited Charles I's son, Charles II, to return to the British throne, which he did in 1660, the date of his 'Restoration'. This is a convenient date at which to divide British history; before 1660 we are in the late-Renaissance world of the Reformation, with its wars and religious controversies, the period of Luther, Queen Elizabeth, Shakespeare and the Puritans. After 1660 we enter the neo-classical, 'Augustan' world of peace, prosperity and polish (at least on the surface), the period of Dryden and Pope, the great age of country houses and a stable society.

Charles II had no legitimate sons and was succeeded by his brother, the Catholic James, Duke of York, who became James II in 1685. A bastard son of Charles II, the Duke of Monmouth, attempted a rebellion from France and Ireland but was unsuccessful in asserting the claims of the Protestant succession and was executed. James II became increasingly unpopular, however, and in 1688 was removed by what would now be known as a 'bloodless coup'. Parliament invited his daughter Mary to become queen with her Dutch Protestant husband, William, as king. Their establishment as 'William and Mary' in 1689, the result of what came to be known as the 'Glorious Revolution', is referred to as the Revolution Settlement. This Settlement re-established a limited Protestant monarchy and hailed an era of stability in Britain that had only one thing to threaten it.

This one thing was the family of the deposed James II, now living in France with his fellow-Catholic King Louis XIV. As long as William and Mary or their daughter Anne (1702–14) were on the throne, the time did not seem ripe for instigating a rebellion, but when Anne died childless the exiled Stuarts, as they were known from the family name of Charles I, felt that the moment had come to attempt to regain the British throne. Parliament, fearing the Catholic Stuarts, invited George, Elector of Hanover, a descendant of King James I, the first Stuart king of England, to take the throne. When he did this in 1714 the country was split into those who thought that this was an admirable repetition of the Revolution Settlement of 1689 (basically the Whig party who had wanted to exclude James II from the succession and who had welcomed William and Mary) and those who thought that the Stuart Pretender (James II's son, another James) should now be called to the throne (basically the Tory party, who had Stuart leanings at least until 1760). The 'Old Pretender' James attempted an invasion of England in 1715, a rebellion generally known as 'the '15' in which a large number of Scottish gentry rallied to the Stuart cause. The rebellion was a failure and George I reigned untroubled until his death in 1727 when George II succeeded him. In 1745 the 'Young Pretender', Prince Charles Edward ('Bonnie Prince Charlie', 'the Chevalier de St George') launched another rebellion again collecting a considerable following in Scotland. His troops marched as far south as Derby but there, finding that the English Jacobite gentry (from 'Jacobus', the Latin for 'James') did not rise in any significant numbers to aid them, the rebellion faltered and began to retreat into the north and Scotland. The Hanoverians, whose patience with the Stuarts was now at an end, sent the Duke of Cumberland with a large army after them. He caught and inflicted a bloody defeat on them at Culloden and the Young Pretender escaped back to France whence no Stuart rebellion again emanated.

Tom Jones (written 1746–8) is set against this background with the main action taking place during the most exciting moments of the 1745 rebellion. Fielding is on the Hanoverian side (as is Tom and, it seems, Allworthy) in favour of maintaining the Protestant George II on the throne of Britain on the grounds that in 'no single instance' have the Hanoverians infringed on the 'liberties' of the British nation. This political view can be connected slightly with Fielding's moral views as expressed in the novel. The Jacobites we meet are Squire Western and Partridge, neither of whom is very well endowed with brains; sensible men, who wish to live in peace and freedom, are better off with the relatively parliamentary Georges than they would be with the autocratic and perhaps fanatical Catholic Stuarts. We get the impression that a Hanoverian Britain is more likely to appeal to the manly, bluff virtues of Tom (in one of his aspects) than the roundabout machinations of a court dominated by Catholics and foreigners. Fielding edited two anti-Jacobite newspapers—the *True Patriot* and the *Jacobite's Journal*.

The above does not summarise all the aspects of eighteenth-century politics relevant to *Tom Jones*, although it is the main framework. Of interest too are the following.

There was a tendency for smaller country squires, especially in the remoter provinces, to be Tories and perhaps Jacobites. They stood for country interests against the Whig Hanoverian aristocrats so disliked by Squire Western, a typical Tory of the period. Tories were also staunch defenders of Anglicanism (in spite of their Jacobite hankerings) against Dissent (Methodism or the 'Presbyterianism' disliked by Western).

Along with patriotic fears of the Frenchness of the Stuarts went real fears about a restoration of the Roman Catholic faith. 'My husband is always so afraid of papishes', says one landlady in the novel. At the other end of the religious spectrum people mistrusted 'enthusiasm' and the ardent religions of Dissent. 'I don't care what religion comes', says the puppet-show man in answer to the landlady, 'provided the Presbyterians are not uppermost; for they are enemies to puppet-shows' (Book 12 Chapter 7).

It will be seen from the above paragraphs that religion and politics were quite inseparable in the earlier eighteenth century.

Notice that Sir Walter Scott's first novel, *Waverley*, published in 1814, is the tale of a young Englishman caught up in the 1745 rebellion and makes an interesting contrast with *Tom Jones*.

Fielding's debt to the classics

The debt

Towards the end of Book 5 Chapter 4, after narrating the incident of Sophia's muff and its profound effect on Tom, Fielding cites the following lines of verse:

Thus the poet sweetly sings of Troy.
—*Captique dolis lachrymisque coacti*
Quos neque Tydides, nec Larissaeus Achilles,
Non anni domuere decem, non mille carinae.

What Diomede, or Thetis' greater son,
A thousand ships, nor ten years siege had done,
False fears, and fawning words, the city won.
Dryden

We can take this as an unmistakable example of the debt Fielding and his contemporaries owed to the classics. Note how Fielding assumes that we know who the 'poet' is—it is Virgil, in fact, referring to Homer's story of the fall of Troy (in the *Iliad*) in his *Aeneid*. We are also expected to know enough of the story to get the point that the winning of Troy was the winning back of Helen (the love-story is apposite to Tom and Sophia here), and to understand who Tydides and Achilles were, and to accept the thousand ships and the ten years (two standard motifs of the Trojan story), and to know what the 'false fears, and fawning words' were (or at least to know how these elements fit into the story). Besides this we are given the Latin so that we can admire or criticise the Dryden translation (and we are told that it *is* Dryden's so that we can compare other versions, perhaps). Thus we have to make the jump between 'Larissaeus Achilles' to 'Thetis' greater son': Achilles was from Larissa, but he was also Thetis' son and Dryden needed that word for his rhyme.

It is hard for us to imagine the extent to which literate eighteenth-century people knew their classics. Fielding is being in no way pretentious when he includes these lines from Virgil and their translation; he is writing for an audience that finds no difficulty in understanding all the points elaborated about this passage above, and dozens more besides. The point is that to a large degree education in Fielding's day simply was a classical one: first the languages and then the literatures of Greece and Rome were studied for years on end at school and university. The results were not bad and certainly the average twentieth-century reader is left somewhat at sea by his ignorance in this direction.

There follow some examples of Fielding's explicit debts to the classics in *Tom Jones*.

Epic similes

In the classical epics (those by Homer and Virgil) extended similes are often used to convey a strong picture of particularly dramatic moments in the story. Fielding employs this device to great effect, imitating the classics faithfully and often writing in that slightly stilted English that can be the product of a close translation from Greek or Latin. The first example in *Tom Jones* appears at the beginning of Book 1 Chapter 6: 'Not otherwise than when a kite, tremendous bird . . .'. The oddity of the English here accurately reflects a Latin original and the whole simile (it occupies an entire paragraph) conjures up a most apt picture of the disturbance Deborah Wilkins is causing in the village.

See also: Book 2 Chapter 4: 'As fair Grimalkin, who . . .'
       Book 5 Chapter 8: 'To say the truth . . .'
       Book 6 Chapter 9: 'As when two doves . . .'
       Book 11 Chapter 6: 'As a miser . . .'
And there are others.

The battle in the churchyard

Book 4 Chapter 8 is called 'A Battle sung by the Muse in the Homerican Style and which none but the classical Reader can taste'. If this chapter is examined it will be seen to possess a number of Fielding's classical elements. First, he invokes the Muses, the goddesses supposed to inspire the arts ('Ye Muses then . . .'). Then he indulges in an epic simile ('As a vast herd of cows . . .'). Next he drops into an epic style of long sentences (the paragraphs beginning 'As a vast herd of cows . . .' and 'Molly, having endeavoured . . .' consist of only five sentences in twenty-eight lines). Next he adopts the epic practice of asking the Muse to list the names of the fallen heroes ('Recount, O Muse . . .') and in this list he gives descriptions of these heroes, or epithets at least, in the Homeric manner, thus 'Old Echepole, the sow-gelder . . . Kate of the Mill . . . Tom Freckle, the smith's son . . . he was an ingenious workman, and made excellent pattins . . .' Besides this there is a deliberately stilted quality in Fielding's English. He writes 'Him the pleasant banks of sweetly winding Stower had nourished, where he first learnt the vocal art', demonstrating classical inversion (putting 'Him' at the beginning rather than at the end of the first part of the sentence) and circumlocution ('vocal art' for 'singing'). This analysis could be continued almost indefinitely.

Fielding tends to use classical devices or slip into a classical tone whenever he wishes to be elevated (as in the description of Sophia in Book 4 Chapter 2, although the 'elevation' of the style is somewhat tongue-in-cheek) or especially ludicrous (as in the battle here discussed or in the battle of Upton in Book 9 Chapter 3).

A prelude to love

In Book 9 Chapter 5 Tom dines with Mrs Waters and ends up by spending the night with her. This act will bring its own punishment (Tom will offend Sophia and not see her) but Fielding wishes it to be considered a peccadillo rather than a serious fault. He inclines to credit good characters with healthy sexual appetites and bad characters, such as Blifil, with an inferior substitute such as love of money. Thus he needs a style which will make the episode attractive, amusing and light-hearted. He adopts a classical tone throughout.

The initial discussion of 'heroes' depends largely on our knowledge of the semi-divine nature of some of the Greek heroes and this is reinforced by the direct comparison between Tom and Ulysses who, in Homer, is a great eater and a great lover, the two qualities of Tom's character we see in action here. After some further discussion of the relationship between food and love, Fielding makes a bow to one of the great Roman love poets, Ovid, and asks the Graces of Greek myth to recount the love-scene that is to follow. This they do in an extended epic simile in which Mrs Waters's designs on Tom are likened to military operations. The result is hilarious.

Fielding, employing mock-epic (or 'mock-heroic') devices rather as Swift and Pope had done a little earlier in the century (Swift's *Battle of the Books* and Pope's *Dunciad*), had at his command a whole range of ways of establishing the proper attitude towards the events of *Tom Jones*. It is not necessary to an enjoyment of the novel for us to pick up every classical hint, but a general awareness of the literature he is reworking for his own purposes seems essential.

Tom Jones and the theatre

Fielding was a dramatist and theatre manager for many years before becoming a novelist. This is reflected in *Tom Jones* in three main ways. In each case it must be remembered that the theatre referred to is the lively but conventional theatre of the Restoration and Augustan periods with its comedy of manners, its satire and its farce (the tragedy of the period is of less direct relevance to *Tom Jones* although Otway and others are referred to by Fielding).

First, then, Fielding's characterisation is somewhat theatrical. His people have strongly marked characters, somewhat fixed in type. Their names often indicate their characters, and their speech always does. This is not uncommon in fiction but in Fielding's case it is marked enough for us to look back at the very similar characterisation in his own plays and in those of his predecessors (Vanbrugh, Wycherley, Etherege and also Molière, among others).

Secondly, Fielding sometimes needs rapid dialogue of a theatrical kind and his talent as a dramatist is evident in the ease with which it flows from his pen. As an example we can take the last paragraph of Book 18 Chapter 12, beginning 'But he soon returned with Allworthy', in which Sophia, Western and Allworthy exchange quick-fire sentences of a sort which could go straight into the dialogue of a play without alteration.

Thirdly, Fielding often develops episodes that depend to some extent on theatrical devices and creates scenes that could be put directly on to a stage. An example here is the uncovering of Square in Molly Seagrim's bedroom, in Book 5 Chapter 5. Square's concealment behind a blanket is highly reminiscent of the many people who are hidden behind screens and doors in comedy and there is also a dramatic touch in that the reader is not told of Square's presence until the blanket drops. In other words the reader is in the position of a member of the audience in a theatre receiving a surprise.

Another example would be the scenes at Upton which read very like a Restoration comedy or farce, complete with mistaken identities and bedroom changes. Besides these, however, it would be worth noting the frequent references Fielding makes to the theatre as, for instance, in the introductory chapter to Book 10 where we read: 'Every person, for instance, can distinguish between Sir Epicure Mammon and Sir Fopling Flutter; but to note the difference between Sir Fopling Flutter and Sir Courtly Nice, requires a more exquisite judgement'. Fielding assumes that we are familiar with the plays by Jonson, Etherege and John Crowne from which these characters are selected. The characters' names imply their fixed type clearly enough.

Part 4

Hints for study

Points for detailed study

Fielding's Introductory Chapters

The first chapter of each of the eighteen books of *Tom Jones* is a direct address to the reader by the author. This device, later widely used, as, for example, by Thackeray and George Eliot, enables Fielding to comment on the action of the novel, to justify his choices and to attack would-be critics. It also gives him the opportunity to elaborate a neo-classical critical theory. These introductory chapters do not advance the plot of the novel and they usually do not even mention any of the characters by name. They show Fielding at his most urbane and Augustan, as well as at his most satirical. They also show the extent of his classical learning and his wide involvement in the life and literature of his age. (See the last paragraph of Book 1 Chapter 2: 'Reader, I think proper . . . to acquaint thee, that I intend to digress'.)

Fielding's irony

The overall tone of *Tom Jones* is ironic. That is to say, in a large number of cases Fielding or his characters say one thing when they mean another or employ a high style when a low one would be more appropriate. Fielding takes a jocular and slightly distant attitude towards his own creations that reinforces this ironic tone.

Thus when Fielding writes 'By means of this wonderful sagacity, Mrs Western had now, as she thought, made a discovery of something in the mind of Sophia' (Book 6 Chapter 2), we understand that her 'sagacity' is only 'wonderful' in the sense that it is wonderfully wrong and that Mrs Western has entirely misunderstood Sophia. Then again, the landlords and landladies of the various inns in the novel express opinions about Tom in direct relation not to how he behaves but to whether they think he is rich or not: when they scent money they praise him and when they scent poverty they abuse him. Or again, Fielding often refers to a 'libation' (wine poured out in honour of the gods) when he means a drink (poured down the throat). These examples, and there are many others, have in common that they all suggest an ironic gap between what is said and what is meant. The connection between this and Fielding's hated vice of hypocrisy is worth examining.

Fielding's ironic distance from his material could be established by a study of the many fights in the novel. Somehow we do not feel the pain of being hit in the face or over the head, or scratched, when these things happen. Our attention is on the brilliance of the formal prose in which they are described. See, for instance, Book 5 Chapter 11.

The character of Mr Allworthy

There is a question in many readers' minds about Mr Allworthy. Is he really 'all-worthy' or has Fielding been misled by his respect for his friend Ralph Allen into praising a character that is full of weaknesses? There are two points to be made here.

First, Fielding throughout *Tom Jones* is well in control of his material and he is rarely ambiguous about moral issues. He is a master of presenting moral character and can do so deftly and accurately. It is therefore probably fair to assume that he knew what he was about in his portrait of Allworthy and that he intended him to appear as he does.

Secondly, Fielding suffers from being unable to fit in completely with the Christian scheme of things, and the trouble here lies in an internal contradiction in the Bible. The God of the Old Testament is a vengeful and wrathful deity whose main attribute lies in his dispensing of justice; Christ, the Son of this stern father, represents mercy, love and charity. In general Jehovah gives people what they *should* get (what they deserve) but Christ proposes that love and forgiveness should be extended to sinners. The difficulty here is that it becomes almost impossible to decide, in individual cases, whether to apply justice or mercy. Allworthy clearly represents the former and Tom the latter, although Fielding is at great pains to stress Allworthy's benevolence and generosity. Thus he is the kindest of uncles to Tom but he does expel him from Paradise Hall as an act of justice.

The implication in the novel seems to be that Allworthy would behave mercifully (towards Tom and towards Partridge, for instance, whom he also expels) if he knew the true facts of the case but that, in his ignorance, he applies justice as he can see no benefit in mercy (Tom and Partridge seem irredeemable). Two questions at once arise: first, as a true Christian should he not *always* be merciful, for to understand everything is to forgive everything? Secondly, if he is all-worthy, what excuse is there for his lamentable ignorance of human nature? The answer to the first question seems to be contained in the person of Tom who is very nearly perfectly charitable, as for instance when he gives two guineas to a man who has tried to rob him. Allworthy would have done better to behave in this generous way himself. The second question is more difficult, for Allworthy really does seem impercipient at times. 'He perfectly well knew mankind', says Fielding when Allworthy has to deal with an irate Squire Western in Book 6 Chapter 10, but it is not true. He misjudges Thwackum and Square, who should really not be allowed to act as tutors to anybody, and he misjudges Jenny Jones and Partridge, Blifil and Dowling, and, of course, Tom.

Fielding attempts to exonerate Allworthy by pointing out that he is deceived by clever enemies (Blifil) and that his credulity stems from a desire to believe what people say. See his conduct towards Jenny Jones at the end of Book 1 Chapter 7. The question can be argued, but it is hard not to agree when Tom (who has learned how the money he gave to the 'highwayman' Anderson has saved his family) reflects with horror 'on the dreadful consequences which must have attended them [Anderson's family], had he listened rather to the voice of strict justice, than to that of mercy when he was attacked on the high road' (Book 13 Chapter 10).

The final problem seems simply to be that Fielding has set up mercy as the great virtue in his novel, and has exemplified it in his hero, but has also included a character who, although called Allworthy, is in fact not completely merciful.

Character revealed in speech

Fielding differentiates his characters by putting different sorts of speech into their mouths. This is one way of approaching the question of his language: he is clearly a master of different accents just as he is a master of varying tones in his descriptive prose.

First there is the west-country speech of Squire Western and the servants and yokels in Somerset. This approximates to the 'oo-arr' west-country accent of yokels on stage and screen today. The perfect Sophia does not have a trace of this accent.

Mrs Honour, and some of the landladies of inns, have a lower-class accent that is not specifically rustic. They tend to muddle up long words and talk in catch-phrases and their accent is hardly that of the fully educated. See, for example, Mrs Honour's speech in Book 4 Chapter 12.

The professional classes tend to speak in a manner suited to their professions. Thus the lawyers talk legal jargon and the doctors medical jargon at the slightest provocation.

Mr Allworthy speaks in dignified and measured tones. Perhaps he is at one end of the spectrum that includes all the *gentlemen*, from Ensign Northerton, with his slang and his swearing, upwards.

Mrs Western talks a kind of sub-diplomatic political jargon; Thwackum's and Square's language lives up to their arrogance and pomposity. In the case of these two last Fielding is at great pains to contrast their words with each other's, with Allworthy's and with reality.

Often people establish their characters with a few sentences, so that they are then set up for a fall if they do not live up to the characters they have given themselves. Thus 'honest Broadbrim', the Quaker, with his Biblical 'thou hasts', is setting himself up for being discovered as an uncharitable hypocrite (Book 7 Chapter 10).

Tom himself, like Sophia, has no accent beyond that of the educated gentry. He is not acting a part (he is not a hypocrite) so there is no need for him to fall into jargon. His speech, like the speech of everyone else in the novel, is a mirror of his personality and as the latter is straightforward, open, kind, free and manly, so is the former.

The structure of *Tom Jones*

Fielding kept a 'calendar' of the events in his novel in order to avoid getting his time sequences mixed up. In fact it will be found that, although there is one small error in Book 18 where Mrs Miller enters a room which she has not left, Fielding's novel 'works' in a practical sense: sufficient time is left for each action or journey and the plot is well crafted.

In addition to this it must have been noticed that there is a symmetrical arrangement of the books of the novel. The first six take us through all the action at Tom's home until he is expelled from it as a young man. The next six take us through Tom's country travels, and those of the others. The final six are set in London.

These mechanical points suggest that Fielding was a careful and accurate writer, concerned to achieve that classical effect of balance so dear to his century. This applies also to some of the less mechanical aspects of the novel. Thwackum is balanced by Square, Tom by Blifil, Allworthy by Western, and so on. Some hard thought about the book will reveal a number of other balances.

Selecting quotations

Many of the best points that can be made about *Tom Jones* can be supported by reference to certain episodes rather than by actual quotation. In these cases a reference to the book and chapter in which the episode occurs should be sufficient as the chapters are generally short.

Thus, to establish Squire Western's impetuosity and obsession with field sports, it would be a good idea to refer to the episode (in Book 12 Chapter 2) in which he abandons his pursuit of Sophia simply because he comes across a hunt in full cry and cannot resist joining it. None the less, quotation is always the most convincing sort of literary evidence,

and for *Tom Jones* most points will be best made by reference to an
episode *and* quotation. Thus, in the example given about Squire
Western, there is nothing very easily quotable in the chapter which
describes his diversion from hunting Sophia to hunting a fox, but we
could pick up a quotable description of the Squire and his impetuosity
from one of the later books of the novel, for instance, from Book 18
Chapter 8, which opens with Western bursting in on Mr Allworthy and
Mrs Waters when they are together, or Book 18 Chapter 9, where Fielding talks of Western, by implication, as being among the men who are
'over-violent in their dispositions'.

This principle of selecting an episode and matching it with a quotation, perhaps from another part of the novel, can be applied particularly to making points about character. Fielding puts everyone into
character-testing situations and these can be clinched with his authorial
comments about the characters that are made elsewhere. Some examples
of this can be given in a table (see below).

This sort of two-pronged attack, using incidents and quotations, can
be applied to everyone in the novel, including Tom himself, of course. As
it is Fielding's intention that every incident should reveal character,
there are plenty of examples to choose from in every case. A simple
demonstration of this appears in Book 5 Chapter 2, where Tom is confined to bed with a broken arm. He is visited by Allworthy, Thwackum,
Square, Western, Blifil and Sophia. They all behave in characteristic

name	episode demonstrating character	quotation supporting the point
Mr Allworthy	His free acceptance of the responsibility of bringing up Tom (Book 1 Chapter 6: 'As to your child . . .') and his support of Mrs Miller in London (Book 18) demonstrate his *generosity*	Book 1 Chapter 3: 'As good-nature had always the ascendant in his mind . . .' Book 1 Chapter 2: Allworthy has 'a benevolent heart'.
Blifil	His malicious behaviour towards Sophia and her pet bird (Book 4 Chapter 3) His poisoning of Mr Allworthy's mind against Tom (throughout the early books of the novel)	Book 3 Chapter 10: 'Master Blifil fell very short of his companion in the amiable quality of mercy.'
Sophia	Her resolve to quit her father's house rather than marry Blifil (Book 7 Chapter 7) and her determination not to marry him even when her father has caught her in London (Book 16 onwards) demonstrate her *strength of mind*	'Such was the outside of Sophia . . .' and the rest of this paragraph at the end of Book 4 Chapter 2

name	episode demonstrating character	quotation supporting the point
Partridge	A good fellow but a weak character, timorous and sometimes greedy His terror of the dark and of the Man of the Hill (Book 8 Chapter 10) But when Jones is attacked in the Battle of Upton, Partridge goes to his rescue (Book 9 Chapter 3) Note his behaviour, in contrast to that of Tom, during the incident of the 'highwayman' (Book 12 Chapter 14)	Book 8 Chapter 9: 'We have already observed that he was a very good-natured fellow, and he hath himself declared the violent attachment he had to the person and character of Jones; but . . .' Book 9 Chapter 3: 'Partridge, though not much addicted to battle, would not however stand still when his friend was attacked . . .'
Lady Bellaston	Her somewhat loose character is redeemed to some degree by her attachment to Tom. For him she is prepared to act a little better than she usually does, but she is really rather immoral. Thus she is prepared to plot and lie and even plan Lord Fellamar's rape of Sophia (Book 15 Chapter 2 onwards)	Book 14 Chapter 2: 'Haughty and amorous as this lady was, she submitted at last to bear the second place . . .' Book 15 Chapter 3: Lady Bellaston is a member of a 'society' in which the rule is that 'every member should, within the twenty-four hours, tell at least one merry fib.' She goes to the length of asking Lord Fellamar 'Are you frighted by the word *rape*? Or are you apprehensive—?' (Book 15 Chapter 4) in order to goad him into action
Thwackum	His charity is only in his mouth, not in his heart (and sometimes not even in his mouth) as in the case of his reaction to Mr Allworthy's legacy when that gentleman thinks he is about to die. Thwackum more or less curses his employer for only leaving him a thousand pounds (in fact a substantial sum) He is antagonistic to sexual behaviour, something which in Fielding is always a sign of a mean spirit (compare Tom himself). See Book 5 Chapter 10, where he catches Tom with Molly	Book 3 Chapter 2: 'Thwackum did all he could to dissuade Allworthy from shewing any compassion or kindness to the boy . . .' Book 18 Chapter 4: Thwackum was 'proud and ill-natured . . . Allworthy did not esteem nor love the man . . .' Book 5 Chapter 10: 'The parson was not only strictly chaste in his own person; but a great enemy to the opposite vice in all others.'

ways which confirm our impression of their natures. Fielding is at his
most obviously moral here.

Besides quotation for the sake of establishing character, most other
quotations will be needed to support points made about Fielding's
moral purposes and about his style. Many of these will be found either
in the notes in Part 2 or in the relevant sections of Part 3.

Fielding writes in a full and sometimes leisurely style and it is often
the case that lengthy quotation seems necessary. This can be abbrevi-
ated by briefly describing the context of the important clause or sentence and then quoting only that. For example, love is clearly a
significant part of the moral structure of the novel, and when we come
to Fielding's discussion of it (Book 6 Chapter 1) we may want to quote
most of the chapter to make our point about this adequately. This would
be impossible, of course, but instead we could summarise the chapter
and quote only its pithiest moments, thus:

> In Book 6 Chapter 1, Fielding presents us with his view of love. He
> says that to look for this most precious commodity in 'the nastiest of
> all places, a bad mind' is absurd and that only good natures will really
> understand love. There are people who do not feel love, and there
> are those who only feel lust, but there are also those with a 'kind and
> benevolent disposition' who can love their fellows and when this is
> joined to sexual desire the result is bliss. Of course, if the reader is not
> prepared to admit of the existence of this tender passion, then read-
> ing more of *Tom Jones* will only be like a 'discourse on colours to a
> man born blind'.

This method of description or summary interspersed with short quotations may be the best way of dealing with Fielding's delightful prolixity.

Specimen questions and answers

(1) Discuss the role of the law in Tom Jones

Fielding was a barrister and a magistrate, concerned to fight crime in
London. (Quote from Introduction to your edition of the novel.)

The novel is concerned with morality, some of which is private (kindness and generosity between individuals) but much of which is public
(poaching; getting bastards). Give examples.

Public morality is, precisely, the area with which the law is concerned.
Black George, Partridge, Jenny Jones, the gypsies, Fitzpatrick, Tom
himself, Lord Fellamar and many others are put into situations where
we can judge their actions morally *and* legally. The two should be the
same and where they are not we can judge the law too. Give examples
(for instance, are the game laws too harsh?).

Law is only as good as the judges who administer it. Even Mr Allworthy is blind to Tom's real virtues so it is not surprising that Squire
Western is an inadequate magistrate or that Dowling is a less than
honest lawyer. Give examples.

Ideally law and morality should go hand in hand with religious principles. Where there is a gap we suspect hypocrisy. For all three areas
(law, morality and religion) the central dilemma is between justice and
mercy. Explain in each case.

Finally, in this moral novel the law is introduced to be tested against
morality and religion, itself to test those who administer it and, of
course, as a machinery for advancing the plot (for example, Tom in
prison because of the duel). In the end this example of the duel shows
up all the problems of the trio law-morality-religion both in the shape
of the central dilemma (justice demands a life for a life but mercy would
save Tom from hanging) and at other levels: honour demands that Tom
fight Fitzpatrick, Christianity forbids it and the law will punish it, yet
morally Tom seems free of guilt. (See especially Book 7 Chapter 9.)

---

(2) Discuss Fielding's range of styles in Tom Jones

Tom Jones is written in a number of styles, although all of them are un-
mistakably Fielding's own. Very few of them are solemn or sentimental.
Most of the novel is written in an ironic and humorous style which
reveals the characters as puppets and the author as the puller of strings,
as in Thackeray's *Vanity Fair* (1847), which was modelled on *Tom
Jones*. But there are different types of humour and irony. Fielding opts
for somewhat fixed characters who each speak in their own way and
about whom he speaks in a style usually elevated in direct proportion
to their vulgarity. Thus the speech of the 'low' people such as Mrs
Honour or the Seagrims is comically vulgar, full of malapropisms and
poor pronunciation, but Fielding will often treat such people in his
most elevated classical style. (See Book 4 Chapters 7 and 8, or Book 7
Chapter 8.) The result is an amusing disparity between what is being
done and the style in which it is being related.

Conversely, Fielding is often at his most simple when he is dealing
with the straightforward behaviour of the better people. Thus Allworthy
stops the lengthy arguments of Thwackum and Square with a simple
sentence (Book 3 Chapter 3) and Squire Western's speech, although
often in dialect, tends to reflect his direct nature.

Besides this matter of the characters' own speech (for which see
'Character revealed in speech', above) Fielding, in his descriptive prose,
tends towards long sentences and a Latin-based vocabulary. Where he
wishes to make an effect he will often descend from this circumlocutory
style to a more direct one in order to show that he is not deafened by his

own verbosity from hearing the truth. These descents are likely to be heralded by 'In short', or '*Viz.*') (See, for example, Book 12 Chapter 7, paragraph opening 'After Partridge . . .'.)

Finally, the point to establish is that Fielding has an unmistakable style (why? Give examples) but that within this he has an amazing range of speech-patterns (accents, dialects, grammar) and several versions of his own descriptive style, varying between more or less elevated, classical and complex.

---

(3) What is the relationship between man's sexual and his moral natures in Tom Jones?

Start at Book 6 Chapter 4, with the paragraph opening 'The charms of Sophia had not made the least impression on Blifil . . .'

Describe how Blifil loves Sophia's money, and loves the idea of taking his revenge on her, perhaps sadistically, after they are married, but how he does not seem capable of frank desire for her. See Book 7 Chapter 6, 'Tho' Mr Blifil . . .' Contrast this with Tom, whose love for Sophia is noble and true and generous but is definitely also sexual. See for instance the end of Book 5 Chapter 2, and the last chapter of the whole novel, in which Tom and Sophia are finally married.

Besides this, Tom is pleasantly lecherous in a way which Fielding makes attractive, although as a Christian he, like Tom, has his qualms about Molly Seagrim, Mrs Waters and Lady Bellaston. Give examples.

Mr Allworthy, significantly, is specifically referred to as having been a somewhat wild youth who had his share of amours; for Fielding this seems essential to a good character. Squire Western is made more endearing by his frank enthusiasm for Tom's 'tousling' of his daughter.

Thwackum, like Blifil, is a cold fish and this is one of the things which make him far less likeable than Square, who at least has enough blood to chase Molly; with success too.

Consider other characters in this light (for instance, Nightingale; the Man of the Hill). Finish perhaps with a reference to Book 6 Chapter 1.

Some other specimen questions

What is the purpose of Fielding's Introductory Chapters?
Discuss Fielding's longer digressions (such as the Man of the Hill's story)
Discuss Fielding's choice of names in *Tom Jones.*
Is Mr Allworthy morally perfect?
Is Tom Jones morally perfect?
Is Fielding a Christian?
Discuss Fielding's method of presenting minor characters.
Discuss the structure of *Tom Jones.*

Part 5

Suggestions for further reading

The text

The best text is that edited by R.P.C. Mutter and available in a Penguin Edition, Penguin Books, Harmondsworth, first published 1966, often reprinted. See Note on the text, Part 1, above.

Other works by Fielding

Shamela (1741)
Joseph Andrews (1742)
> (Published together, Oxford University Press, London, 1971, ed. Douglas Brooks. Also in Everyman's Library, ed. A.R. Humphreys, Dent, London, 1962 and 1973. *Joseph Andrews* is published separately, for instance by Signet Classics, New York, 1961, and by Penguin Books, Harmondsworth, 1977.)

Jonathan Wild (1743)
> (Everyman's Library) ed. A.R. Humphreys, Dent, London, 1964.

Amelia (1752)
> (Everyman's Library) ed. A.R. Humphreys, Dent, London, 2 vols, 1962.

These are Fielding's novels—if we can include the part-biography *Jonathan Wild* in that category—and thus represent only part of his work, albeit the major part. For a list of his plays, periodicals and other writings see, for instance, the A.R. Humphreys edition of *Shamela* and *Joseph Andrews* mentioned above or any bibliography.

Critical and general reading

COMPTON, NEIL (ED): *Henry Fielding: Tom Jones* (*Casebook* series), Macmillan, London, 1970
DUDDEN, F.H.: *Henry Fielding, His Life, Works and Times*, Clarendon Press, Oxford, 1952
EHRENPREIS, IRVIN: *Tom Jones* (*Studies in English Literature* series), Edward Arnold, London, 1964

HARRISON, BERNARD: *Henry Fielding's Tom Jones: The Novelist as Moral Philosopher* (*Text and Context* series), Sussex University Press, London, 1975

HASSALL, A.J.: *Henry Fielding's Tom Jones*, Sydney University Press, Sydney, 1979

PAULSON, R. and LOCKWOOD, T. (EDS): *Henry Fielding: The Critical Heritage*, Routledge, London, 1969

RAWSON, C.J.: *Henry Fielding: A Critical Anthology*, Penguin Books, Harmondsworth, 1973

WATT, IAN: *The Rise of the Novel*, Chatto, London, 1957; Penguin Books, Harmondsworth, 1963

The author of these notes

LANCE ST JOHN BUTLER was educated at Pembroke College, Cambridge. He taught English in Iraq, Algeria and London before working for a year as a banker in Brazil. He was a lecturer in English at King Abdulaziz University, Jeddah, Saudi Arabia (1970–71), then a post-graduate student at the University of East Anglia (1971–72) before becoming a lecturer at the University of Stirling in 1972. He has edited *Thomas Hardy after Fifty Years* (1977) and written *Thomas Hardy* (1978).

The first 100 titles

CHINUA ACHEBE	*Arrow of God* *Things Fall Apart*
JANE AUSTEN	*Northanger Abbey* *Pride and Prejudice* *Sense and Sensibility*
ROBERT BOLT	*A Man For All Seasons*
CHARLOTTE BRONTË	*Jane Eyre*
EMILY BRONTË	*Wuthering Heights*
ALBERT CAMUS	*L'Etranger (The Outsider)*
GEOFFREY CHAUCER	*Prologue to the Canterbury Tales* *The Franklin's Tale* *The Knight's Tale* *The Nun's Priest's Tale* *The Pardoner's Tale*
SIR ARTHUR CONAN DOYLE	*The Hound of the Baskervilles*
JOSEPH CONRAD	*Nostromo*
DANIEL DEFOE	*Robinson Crusoe*
CHARLES DICKENS	*David Copperfield* *Great Expectations*
GEORGE ELIOT	*Adam Bede* *Silas Marner* *The Mill on the Floss*
T.S. ELIOT	*The Waste Land*
WILLIAM FAULKNER	*As I Lay Dying*
F. SCOTT FITZGERALD	*The Great Gatsby*
E.M. FORSTER	*A Passage to India*
ATHOL FUGARD	*Selected Plays*

MRS GASKELL	*North and South*
WILLIAM GOLDING	*Lord of the Flies*
OLIVER GOLDSMITH	*The Vicar of Wakefield*
THOMAS HARDY	*Jude the Obscure* *Tess of the D'Urbervilles* *The Mayor of Casterbridge* *The Return of the Native* *The Trumpet Major*
L.P. HARTLEY	*The Go-Between*
ERNEST HEMINGWAY	*For Whom the Bell Tolls* *The Old Man and the Sea*
ANTHONY HOPE	*The Prisoner of Zenda*
RICHARD HUGHES	*A High Wind in Jamaica*
THOMAS HUGHES	*Tom Brown's Schooldays*
HENRIK IBSEN	*A Doll's House*
HENRY JAMES	*The Turn of the Screw*
BEN JONSON	*The Alchemist* *Volpone*
D.H. LAWRENCE	*Sons and Lovers* *The Rainbow*
HARPER LEE	*To Kill a Mocking-Bird*
SOMERSET MAUGHAM	*Selected Short Stories*
HERMAN MELVILLE	*Billy Budd* *Moby Dick*
ARTHUR MILLER	*Death of a Salesman* *The Crucible*
JOHN MILTON	*Paradise Lost I & II*
SEAN O'CASEY	*Juno and the Paycock*
GEORGE ORWELL	*Animal Farm* *Nineteen Eighty-four*
JOHN OSBORNE	*Look Back in Anger*
HAROLD PINTER	*The Birthday Party*
J.D. SALINGER	*The Catcher in the Rye*

SIR WALTER SCOTT

Ivanhoe
Quentin Durward

WILLIAM SHAKESPEARE

A Midsummer Night's Dream
Antony and Cleopatra
Coriolanus
Cymbeline
Hamlet
Henry IV Part I
Henry V
Julius Caesar
King Lear
Macbeth
Measure for Measure
Othello
Richard II
Romeo and Juliet
The Merchant of Venice
The Tempest
The Winter's Tale
Troilus and Cressida
Twelfth Night

GEORGE BERNARD SHAW

Androcles and the Lion
Arms and the Man
Caesar and Cleopatra
Pygmalion

RICHARD BRINSLEY SHERIDAN

The School for Scandal

JOHN STEINBECK

Of Mice and Men
The Grapes of Wrath
The Pearl

ROBERT LOUIS STEVENSON

Kidnapped
Treasure Island

JONATHAN SWIFT

Gulliver's Travels

W.M. THACKERAY

Vanity Fair

MARK TWAIN

Huckleberry Finn
Tom Sawyer

VOLTAIRE

Candide

H.G. WELLS

The History of Mr Polly
The Invisible Man
The War of the Worlds

OSCAR WILDE

The Importance of Being Earnest